HOLIDAYS

HOLIDAYS

RECIPES, GIFTS AND DECORATIONS

thanksgiving
& christmas

CLARKSON POTTER / PUBLISHERS
NEW YORK

Copyright © 1993 Time Publishing
Ventures
Rockefeller Center, New York,
New York, 10020-1393.

Originally published in book form by
Time Warner in 1993. Published
simultaneously by Clarkson N. Potter,
Oxmoor House, Inc., and Leisure Arts.

The recipes and photographs in this
work were previously published in
MARTHA STEWART LIVING.

Manufactured in the United States
of America.

*Library of Congress
Cataloging-in-Publication Data*
Stewart, Martha
Holidays: favorite recipes, gifts, and
decorations, Thanksgiving through
Christmas/Martha Stewart
p. cm.
Includes index.
1. Holiday cookery. 2. Holiday
decorations. 3. Entertaining.
I. Title
TX739.S76 1994 641.5'68—dc20
94-8638 CIP

ISBN 0-517-88271-X

Designed by
JENNIFER NAPIER

Dedicated
to the readers of
MARTHA STEWART LIVING
magazine

Acknowledgments

THIS BOOK IS BASED ON THREE YEARS OF MARTHA STEWART LIVING MAGAZINE, AND ON THE IDEAS AND HARD, HARD WORK OF MANY PEOPLE.

At the magazine: Eric Thorkilsen, Isolde Motley, Gael Towey, Anne Morgan, Catherine Barnett, Linda Nardi, Lisa Wagner, Laura Harrigan, Donna Agajanian, John Gilliland, Suzie Chu, Wayne Wolf, Tamara Westmark, David Steward, Karen Doyle, Boris Pozin, Bill Walsh, Sarah Medford, Susan Spungen, Valerie Cox, Jennifer Waverek, Amy Schuler, Hannah Milman, Leah Lococo, Eugenia Leftwich, Robert Valentine, Lauren Stanich, Laurel Reed, Peter Mark, Wanda Lau, Celia Barbour, Anne Johnson, Jacqueline Parisier, Schuyler Hoyt, Darcy Miller, Sara Ruffin, Dora Cardinale, Marc Einsele, Susan Wyland, Jennifer Napier, Page Marchese, Adrienne Ledden, Colby Zintl, and Darren Crawforth.

At my home and at my office in Westport, Connecticut: Laura Herbert Plimpton, Alexis Stewart, Necy Fernandes, Renato and Renaldo Abreu, Marie Mendez, Carolyn Kelly, Rita Christiansen, and Julie Cook.

At Oxmoor House in Birmingham, Alabama: Bruce Akin, Nancy Fitzpatrick, John McIntosh, Rick Litton, Cindy Thigpen, and Dianne Mooney. At Capitol Engraving in Nashville, Tennessee: Warren Denney.

For their beautiful photographs: William Abranowicz, Jerry Simpson, Elizabeth Zeschin, Antoine Bootz, Jon Jensen, John Dugdale, Victoria Pearson, Todd Eberle, and Maria Robledo.

For their inspiration and support: Ina Garten, Patti Paige, Marla Weinhoff, Daniel Shaw, Melissa Neufeld, Wendy Dubit, Elizabeth Ryan, Sophie Herbert, Anita Calero, Jeanne White, and Jerry Bolduan.

Contents

Introduction

THE HOLIDAY ISSUES OF OUR MAGAZINE ARE ALWAYS THE MOST CHALLENGING TO PLAN AND EXECUTE. STORIES THAT WILL APPEAR IN NOVEMBER AND DECEMBER MUST BE PHOTOGRAPHED IN AUGUST AND SEPTEMBER, WHEN PUMPKINS ARE HARD TO COME BY, AND THE PROSPECT OF LUGGING PRICKLY SPRUCE AND HOLLY, ROASTING GEESE, AND BAKING BUCHE DE NOEL has little appeal. Jeff Stevens, my family attorney, still regales friends with the story of how I persuaded him to eat a Christmas dinner that was to appear on video while wearing a sweater and tweed jacket—in mid-August, in my home, without air-conditioning. Between takes, he peeled off the top layers and stood in front of a huge fan in my kitchen.

Every year someone makes the case for putting together the magazine a year ahead so we will be synchronized with the seasons. But frankly, long-term planning has never been my forte—like many people, I am more creative and productive with a sense of immediacy. So every year finds us dyeing Easter eggs in January, wearing straw hats and sun dresses in April, and, again, twining pine garlands around the porch columns on Labor Day.

It's difficult to summon up ideas for wreaths or cookies when you long to be at the beach, but somehow, inspiration takes hold, and one day I find the entire staff crowded around the big worktable making ornaments and gift boxes. Inspiration comes from everywhere: As people wander in and out of the office, they contribute memories of childhood rituals, and dreams of the perfect holiday. We find ideas in local antiques stores, in the flower markets, from new friends.

When it comes time to shoot, we forget the season. As photographers, writers, and designers hang swags, look for errant glass balls, cut out cookies, and wrap gifts, they remind me of my brothers and sisters scurrying to finish everything by Christmas Eve. Just "creating" a holiday makes our diverse group into a family.

Our holiday issues, as a result, have a very special feeling to them. They tend to sell out quickly (we still receive daily requests for our first holiday issue, our premiere, but the last copy went long ago). They inspire more letters—many with wonderful personal stories—than other issues. Among our office reference sets, the holiday issues are always the most dog-eared and annotated; sometimes faint sprinklings of flour or sugar fall from between their pages. When the real holiday times come, our homes bear traces of the most recent issue: the art director's tree is topped by a starfish, relic of the time we made ornaments from shells; everyone makes rubber-stamped gift tags; and many of our friends have come to rely on annual baskets of homemade shortbread and preserves.

Inspired by your letters and our own needs, we have decided to gather the best of our holiday issues into one volume so that we would have all the information we need at Thanksgiving and Christmas in one place. The recipes and ideas chosen are those we have used over and over ourselves. We have baked these cookies with our children, hung these wreaths on our own front doors, and served these menus to our friends and families. These are the ways in which we celebrate Thanksgiving and Christmas; we hope that you and your family will share those holidays with us.

Martha Stewart

and THE EDITORS OF MARTHA STEWART LIVING

Thanksgiving Dinner

MENU

Red Pepper Vegetable Soup

Quail with Brussels Sprouts and Shallots

Winter Vegetable Puree

Ina Garten's Cornbread-Stuffed Turkey Breast

Roast Fennel

Garlic Roast Potatoes

Roast Guinea Fowl

Ina's Cornmeal-Cheddar Scones

Kathleen's Brownies

Ina's Apple Crisp

Kathleen's Lemon Bars

WHEN THE FIRST COLONISTS ARRIVED HERE FROM *England, they brought with them the harvest home festival, the feast following the harvest of the last grain. There was no grain (so no pie) at the earliest Thanksgivings, but there were fall's last fruits and vegetables—corn, cranberries, and pumpkins. Wild turkeys, native to the new land, were plentiful too. Four hundred years later, the ingredients for the Thanksgiving menu vary little from the original: by such traditions our histories are transmitted from one generation to the next.*

RIGHT: The symbol of autumn, an Atlantic Giant pumpkin awaiting the harvest. LEFT: A Thanksgiving buffet. Martha covered her table with plastic sheeting, then with sheets of moss from the woods near her home. Pieces of fallen log, leaves, and mushrooms were the decorations. The meal began with Red Pepper Vegetable Soup, served in a tureen made from a scooped out, marbleized pumpkin.

PHOTOGRAPHS BY ANTOINE BOOTZ

We stuffed our quail, above, with savory couscous, our guinea fowl with wild rice and dried apples, and our turkey breast with cornbread, but all of the stuffings are interchangeable as you choose.

Red Pepper Vegetable Soup

SERVES 8 TO 12

The roasted red peppers lend this soup a wonderful, smoky taste and its gorgeous, rosy red tinge.

6   Red bell peppers, roasted (see directions below)
8   tablespoons (1 stick) unsalted butter
2   large onions, chopped
2   cloves garlic, minced
4   large carrots, peeled and chopped
1   large baking potato, peeled and chopped
2   firm, ripe pears, peeled and chopped
5   cups rich chicken stock
1   tablespoon chopped fresh parsley
    Salt and freshly ground pepper
    Crème fraîche (see page 22) or sour cream and
    fresh herb sprigs, for garnish

1. Roast and peel peppers. Halve, seed, and chop flesh.
2. Melt butter in a large pot; add onion and garlic and sauté for 10 minutes. Add carrots, potato, and red pepper; sauté 10 more minutes. Add pears, chicken stock, and parsley. Bring to a boil and simmer 20 minutes, until vegetables are just tender. Season with salt and pepper.
3. Puree soup in batches in a food processor. Return to pot and reheat. Serve garnished with crème fraîche or sour cream and herbs.

HOW TO ROAST A PEPPER

Any kind of pepper–hot or sweet–can be roasted by this method and will taste much better than canned or bottled roast peppers.

1. Holding peppers with long-handled tongs, roast directly over a high gas flame or under a broiler, turning peppers so they get black all over.
2. Wrap each pepper in a paper towel, place in plastic bags, and "sweat" for 15 minutes.
3. Rub off skins with paper towel, then prepare peppers as directed in recipe.

Quail with Brussels Sprouts and Shallots

SERVES 8

Boning a quail may seem like finicky work, but the result—a delicate mouthful—well repays the effort.

8   quail, washed and patted dry
2   cups Couscous Stuffing (recipe follows)
1   quart brussels sprouts, peeled
3   tablespoons olive oil
16   large shallots, peeled
4   sprigs fresh thyme
1   cup dry white wine

1. Bone quail by placing each on a board, breast side down, and cutting along both sides of backbone with a sharp knife or scissors. Cut meat from rib cage, and pull entire carcass from meat. Cut out thigh bones.
2. With the quail skin side down, spoon about 3 tablespoons of stuffing onto meat. "Sew" the back of each quail with a bamboo skewer and truss with butcher's twine.
3. Heat oven to 350°.
4. Blanch brussels sprouts in boiling water for 5 minutes; drain, and set aside.
5. Heat olive oil in a large, heavy skillet. Brown quail in skillet for 5 to 7 minutes, turning from time to time. Remove quail from skillet; add shallots and sauté for 8 to 10 minutes, adding more oil if necessary. Place quail in roasting pan and surround with sprouts, shallots, and thyme. Add wine.
6. Roast for 30 minutes.

COUSCOUS STUFFING

1½ cups chicken stock
1   tablespoon olive oil
6   scallions, chopped (with green tops)
1   clove garlic, minced
1   cup uncooked couscous
1   tablespoon curry powder
¼   teaspoon turmeric
¼   teaspoon cayenne pepper
1   teaspoon salt

1. Heat chicken stock to boiling. Set aside.
2. Heat olive oil in a large skillet. Add scallions and garlic; sauté until soft. Add couscous and stir. Add spices and salt; sauté for 1 to 2 minutes. Add hot chicken stock, remove from heat, and let stand until the liquid has been absorbed and couscous is tender, 10 to 15 minutes.

Winter Vegetable Puree

SERVES 8 TO 12

Most root vegetables—and pumpkins—can serve as the basis for a puree; an apple or pear added while sautéing enhances the flavor.

4   tablespoons (½ stick) unsalted butter
1   1-pound butternut squash, peeled, seeded, and chopped
4   parsnips, peeled and chopped
2   medium onions, peeled and diced
6   carrots, peeled and chopped
2   firm, ripe pears, peeled, cored, and chopped
¼   teaspoon freshly grated nutmeg
     Salt and freshly ground pepper

1. Melt butter in a large skillet. Sauté vegetables and pears for 20 to 25 minutes, until tender. Add a little water if necessary to prevent sticking.
2. Puree mixture in a food processor. Stir in nutmeg and season to taste.

Ina told us how to cut the tops from fist-size pumpkins, fill with winter purée, drizzle with olive oil, and bake for half an hour. As the big pumpkin provides a focus for the buffet, the tiny ones center a dinner plate.

Ina Garten's Cornbread Stuffed Turkey Breast

SERVES 8 TO 12

For smaller gatherings, turkey breast is a splendid alternative to the traditional bird. Easier to carve, too.

4   Red bell peppers, roasted (see page 16)
1   6½-pound fresh turkey breast, boned, with the skin on
4   cups Cornbread Stuffing (recipe follows)
3   tablespoons unsalted butter
¼   teaspoon salt
    Pinch of freshly ground pepper
1   tablespoon each chopped fresh basil, oregano, and thyme

1. Roast and peel peppers as directed. Halve, seed, and chop.
2. Heat oven to 375°.
3. Lay turkey breast flat, skin side down. Spread with half the stuffing, a layer of red peppers, and remaining stuffing. Roll the turkey breast, folding sides toward the middle. Fasten with bamboo skewers and tie with butcher's twine. Lay turkey breast, seam down, on a foil-lined roasting pan. Melt butter and brush on turkey; sprinkle with salt, pepper, and chopped herbs.
4. Roast for 1½ hours, or until nicely browned.

NOTE: This recipe and many of those following are adapted from those of Ina Garten, at the Barefoot Contessa in Easthampton, New York.

INA'S CORNBREAD

8   tablespoons (1 stick) unsalted butter
½   cup buttermilk
3   tablespoons milk
1   large egg
1½ cups sifted all-purpose flour
½   cup granulated sugar
½   cup yellow cornmeal
1   tablespoon baking powder
1   teaspoon salt

1. Heat oven to 325°.
2. Melt butter. Combine with buttermilk, milk, and egg. Sift together dry ingredients; add to buttermilk mixture and stir until just blended. Pour into buttered 10-by-7-inch dish.
3. Bake for 35 to 45 minutes, until firm and golden.

CORNBREAD STUFFING

½   cup (1 stick) unsalted butter
1   cup chopped onion
3   stalks celery, diced (including leaves)
3   tablespoons chopped Italian flat-leaf parsley
5   cups Ina's Cornbread (see left), crumbled
½   cup chicken stock
    Salt and freshly ground pepper

Melt butter in a large skillet; add onions and sauté until soft. Combine with remaining ingredients, mixing well.

Roast Fennel

SERVES 8 TO 12

The anise-flavored fennel bulb has become a familiar salad ingredient; in Europe, though, it is often braised or roasted.

6   large bulbs fennel, trimmed
¼   cup olive oil
    Salt and freshly ground pepper
1   cup grated Parmesan

1. Heat oven to 400°.
2. Blanch whole fennel bulbs in boiling water for 10 minutes and drain. Halve bulbs lengthwise; arrange in a roasting pan, cut side down. Drizzle with olive oil and season to taste.
3. Roast for 20 minutes. Sprinkle with cheese. Return to oven and roast for another 10 to 20 minutes.

Garlic Roast Potatoes

SERVES 8 TO 12

Before roasting potatoes, it is essential to dry them well.

3   pounds small red, yellow, or white potatoes, quartered
¾   cup olive oil
4   tablespoons (½ stick) unsalted butter, melted
12   cloves garlic, minced
    Salt and freshly ground pepper
    Flat-leaf parsley, for garnish

1. Heat oven to 400°.
2. Toss ingredients together and spread on a roasting pan. Roast for 30 to 40 minutes, tossing occasionally, until potatoes are brown and just tender. Garnish with flat-leaf parsley.

Roast Guinea Fowl

SERVES 8

Cornish game hens can be substituted for the guinea hens we used in this recipe. Reduce the roasting time to one hour, total.

3 2½-pound guinea fowl
4 cups Wild Rice Stuffing (recipe follows)
12 leaves flat-leaf parsley
4 tablespoons (½ stick) unsalted butter
  Salt and freshly ground pepper
  Bunch of fresh chervil
  Bunch of fresh parsley
8 cloves garlic, unpeeled
1 cup dry white wine

1. Heat oven to 450°.
2. Wash birds and pat dry. Gently loosen skin of each fowl's breast and place 4 flat-leaf parsley leaves under it. Fill birds with stuffing, truss with butcher's twine, and place in a foil-lined roasting pan. Melt butter and brush birds; sprinkle with salt, pepper, chervil, and parsley, and surround with garlic.

3. Roast for 15 minutes. Add wine to pan and brush birds again with melted butter. Reduce heat to 400° and roast for 1 hour. Cover with foil and roast for 15 to 30 minutes more.

WILD RICE STUFFING

6 ounces wild rice
4 tablespoons (½ stick) unsalted butter
1 medium onion, finely chopped
2 cloves garlic, finely minced
½ cup chopped dried apricots
2 oranges, peeled and chopped
½ cup chopped dried apples
½ cup dried currants
1 tablespoon chopped fresh sage
1 tablespoon chopped fresh chervil
  Salt and freshly ground pepper

1. Cook rice in boiling water for 40 minutes, until just tender.
2. Melt butter in a large skillet; sauté onion and garlic until tender. Add remaining ingredients except for rice and heat through. Add cooked rice, and season with salt and pepper.

Ina's Cornmeal Cheddar Scones

SERVES 8 TO 12

*A basket of homemade scones or good bread on the table takes
little effort and enhances any meal.*

1	cup yellow cornmeal
4	cups sifted all-purpose flour
2	tablespoons baking powder
1½	teaspoons salt
2	tablespoons sugar
1¼	cups (2½ sticks) unsalted butter, cut into pieces
4	large eggs
¾	cup heavy cream
½	cup finely grated cheddar cheese
1	egg beaten with 2 tablespoons heavy cream, for glaze

1. Heat oven to 350°.
2. Sift together dry ingredients. Cut in butter until mixture
resembles coarse meal. Lightly beat eggs with cream and
cheddar cheese, and stir into flour-butter mixture.
3. On a surface dusted with cornmeal, roll out dough to ¾
inch. Cut with a biscuit cutter and place on a parchment-
lined baking sheet. Brush with egg glaze.
4. Bake for 10 minutes, until lightly browned.

**LEFT: Roast, stuffed guinea fowl fresh from the oven. BELOW: When
the pumpkin tureen is full, be sure to support it well from the base.**

PAINTED PUMPKINS

At Thanksgiving, we decorate the table as
well as the front steps with pumpkins. We
use a huge one, hollowed out, as a soup
tureen. (Remember to warm it in the oven
before filling with soup, and transport the
filled pumpkin on a platter, not in your
hands.) We also use small pumpkins in
centerpieces, and sometimes we gild or
marbleize them to fit with a color theme.

To marbleize a pumpkin, fill a wash-
tub with cold water. Drizzle oil-based
paint on the water's surface and swirl
gently. Choose a pumpkin with stem
intact (you'll need it to serve as a handle)
and scrub well. Push the pumpkin down
into the water, then lift up through the
floating paint. Turn pumpkin until all
sides are decorated, then quickly lift out.
Skim water with newspaper to remove
paint, then repeat the process with another color. (We used gold, green, and copper.) Dry the pumpkin overnight. If you
plan to hollow the pumpkin, gild or marbleize it first, let dry, and handle carefully.

HOMEMADE CREME FRAICHE

Several of our recipes call for crème fraîche, which can be hard to find and quite expensive in stores. To make your own, heat 2 cups of heavy cream to 100°. Mix in 2 tablespoons buttermilk or sour cream. Place in a jar, cover, and let sit at room temperature for 6 to 8 hours. Chill until thickened. The mixture will keep, refrigerated, for 2 to 3 weeks. It makes a delicious topping for fruit pies and other desserts, a garnish for soups, and can even stand in for clotted cream at afternoon teas.

Kathleen's Brownies

MAKES 16

Rather than just cutting them into plain squares, shape brownies and bars with cookie or biscuit cutters. It takes no more effort, and makes a charming effect.

5¼ tablespoons unsalted butter
⅔ cup sugar
2 tablespoons water
1 teaspoon vanilla extract
3 cups semisweet chocolate chips
2 large eggs
¾ cup sifted all-purpose flour
¼ teaspoon baking soda
¼ teaspoon salt

1. Heat oven to 325°. Butter a 9-inch-square glass baking dish.
2. Heat butter, sugar, and water until boiling. Combine vanilla and 2 cups of the chocolate chips in a bowl; add hot butter-sugar mixture. Add eggs one at a time, mixing well. Sift together flour, baking soda, and salt; stir into chocolate mixture. Add remaining chocolate chips. Pour into prepared dish.
3. Bake for 35 to 45 minutes, or until slightly firm. Cool and cut into squares or, using biscuit cutters, into rounds.
NOTE: This recipe and the Lemon Bars on page 24 were adapted from *Kathleen's Bake Shop Cookbook*.

Ina's Apple Crisp

SERVES 8 TO 12

The sour cherries and cranberries give this crisp depth of flavor and a lovely pink tint.

16 tart baking apples, peeled, cored, and sliced
¼ pound dried sour cherries, pitted
12 ounces fresh cranberries

1½ teaspoons cinnamon
½ teaspoon ground cloves
1 cup granulated sugar
¼ cup fresh lemon juice
  Grated rind of 1 lemon

TOPPING

1 cup quick-cooking rolled oats
1 cup sifted all-purpose flour
1 cup firmly packed light brown sugar
12 tablespoons (1½ sticks) unsalted butter, very cold and cut into small pieces

1. Heat oven to 350°.
2. Combine filling ingredients; toss well. Mound in a deep, buttered 10-inch-round baking dish.
3. In a food processor, combine topping ingredients and process until it resembles coarse crumbs. Sprinkle over filling.
4. Bake for 60 to 70 minutes; serve with Honey-Vanilla Crème Fraîche (recipe follows).

INA'S HONEY-VANILLA CREME FRAICHE

MAKES 2½ CUPS

2 cups crème fraîche (see above)
1 vanilla bean
⅓ cup honey
1 tablespoon vanilla extract

1. Make crème fraîche and chill for 24 hours, until thick.
2. Cut the vanilla bean in half lengthwise and scrape out the tiny seeds; discard bean. Combine seeds with crème fraîche, honey, and vanilla extract; whip until soft peaks form.

Depression-glass
pedestals carry trufflelike
brownies and lemon-bar
hearts. A rosy apple crisp
sits in a puddle of crème
fraîche on the palest-blue
paste plate.

Kathleen's Lemon Bars

MAKES 32

This is a particularly tangy version of an old favorite.

¾   cup (1½ sticks) unsalted butter, softened
1½ cups sifted all-purpose flour
⅓   cup sugar

TOPPING

4   large eggs
5   tablespoons all-purpose flour
2   cups sugar
¾   cup fresh lemon juice

1. Heat oven to 350°.
2. Combine butter, flour, and sugar. Press mixture into unbuttered 13-by-9-inch pan.
3. Bake for 20 minutes, until just turning brown.
4. For topping, lightly whisk eggs. Sift together flour and sugar; add to eggs. Add lemon juice, stir, and pour over partially baked base.
5. Bake for 20 minutes more, or until topping is firm. Chill before cutting.

BELOW AND RIGHT: The familiar round, orange pumpkin is actually a member of the squash family. Other shapes and colors of squash can also be carved and decorated for the fall holidays.

GROWING GIANT PUMPKINS

Giant-pumpkin seeds can't tolerate cold, says Howard Dill, who breeds and sells Atlantic Giant pumpkin seeds in Nova Scotia. They should be germinated indoors in early spring at seventy degrees Fahrenheit; seedlings can be planted in the ground once all danger of frost is past. Giant pumpkins need room to grow—seedlings must be planted at least twenty feet apart—and they thrive with a fair amount of sunshine, moderate temperatures, light soil, and composted manure for fertilizer.

Male flowers appear first, in early summer, followed by females, each bearing a tiny pumpkin, which will not grow unless the flower is fertilized. Growers intent on championship pumpkins should hand-fertilize the female blossom with the male stamen early the morning that the female blooms. When the baby pumpkins are the size of oranges, remove from each vine all but one or two good ones close to the stem. In midsummer, slide a board under each pumpkin to protect it from damp soil. As they approach full size, giant pumpkins can gain ten to fifteen pounds a day—and they'll tear away from their stems if the vine isn't loosened from the soil. They'll also consume a lot of water—or milk, a secret some champion pumpkin growers swear by.

Perfect Pies

FOR THOSE WHO DID NOT GROW UP MAKING PIES AT *mother's side, the perfect crust seems elusive. But the rules are simple.* One: *Use good, unbleached all-purpose flour and fresh unsalted butter.* Two: *Keep all pastry ingredients cold.* Three: *Handle the dough as little as possible (the food processor is a boon).* Four: *Chill the dough before rolling.* Five: *Roll on a cold surface, and brush off excess flour from board, pin, and pastry.* Six: *For a crisp bottom crust, use an old-fashioned metal pie tin.* Seven: *Fill with ripe, unblemished fruit—save the windfalls for apple butter.* Eight: *Heat the oven before putting in the pie.* Nine: *Bake until the juices bubble.* Ten: *Bake often. It is as easy as pie.*

LEFT: An antique pie rack piled high with lemon meringue pies. RIGHT: Martha's niece Sophie made (and devoured) an apple pie with a pâte brisée crust and latticed top. It looked, and tasted, perfect.

PHOTOGRAPHS BY JOHN DUGDALE

A lattice-topped apple pie cools on an antique wooden rack. Pies should cool for an hour to allow the crust to set and juices to thicken.

Apple Pie

SERVES 10 TO 11

Here are three pastry treatments for our classic American dessert.

1	recipe Pâte Brisée (see box at right)
8	tart apples, peeled, cored, and cut into 1-inch chunks or thinly sliced
½	cup sugar
	Juice of ½ lemon
1	teaspoon cinnamon
¼	teaspoon ground cloves
	Pinch of nutmeg
1	tablespoon all-purpose flour
2	tablespoons cold unsalted butter, cut into small pieces
1	large egg beaten with 2 tablespoons heavy cream, for egg glaze
	Sugar, for sprinkling on top

1. For a double-crust pie, roll out half the dough to a thickness of ⅛ inch and use to line a 9-inch pie tin, leaving a 1-inch overhang. Roll out remaining dough to a diameter of 12 inches. Chill both crusts, covered, until firm, at least 30 minutes.
2. Heat oven to 375°. In a large bowl, toss together apples, sugar, lemon juice, spices, and flour. Spoon into chilled pie shell, dot with butter, and cover with remaining pastry circle. Cut several several steam vents across top. Seal by crimping edges. Brush pastry with egg glaze and sprinkle with sugar. Bake for 50 to 60 minutes, or until pastry is golden brown and juices are bubbling. Let cool on wire rack before serving.

FREE-FORM BOTTOM-CRUST VARIATION

Combine dough halves. Roll out to a 14-inch circle ⅛ inch thick. Transfer to a parchment-lined baking sheet and chill, covered, until firm, at least 30 minutes. Prepare filling as directed in step 2 above, and place in center of pastry. Bring up dough over filling. Glaze and bake as directed.

LATTICE-TOP VARIATION

Roll out half the dough to a thickness of ⅛ inch and use to line a 9-inch pie tin, leaving a 1-inch overhang. Roll out remaining dough to a large circle and cut as many strips as possible using a fluted pastry wheel or a sharp knife. Weave lattice as directed in step 10 on the following page. Chill top and bottom crusts, covered, until firm, at least thirty minutes. Prepare filling as directed in step 2 above. Carefully transfer lattice to top of pie, trimming off excess dough and attaching ends using ice water. Glaze and bake as directed.

Pâte Brisée

MAKES TWO 10-INCH CRUSTS

Store pastry rounds tightly wrapped in the freezer (they will keep for a month) for quick pies and tarts.

2½	cups all-purpose flour
1	teaspoon salt
1	teaspoon sugar
½	pound (2 sticks) cold unsalted butter, cut into small pieces
½	cup ice water

1. Place flour, salt, and sugar in bowl of a food processor. Add butter and process for 10 seconds, or just until mixture resembles a coarse meal.
2. With machine running, add ice water, drop by drop. Stop as soon as dough holds together, even if there is water left over. Better the dough be a little crumbly than wet or sticky.
3. Divide dough in half and turn out onto two large pieces of plastic wrap. Press dough into flat circles, wrap in plastic, and chill for at least a hour, or freeze for later use.

ASSEMBLING A PIE

Anyone can make a perfect pie, says Martha, who instructs her niece Sophie in the art of making the classic apple variety.

1. Sophie uses a food processor to cut butter into the flour, while Martha attempts to catch up with an ordinary pastry blender.

2. Sophie finishes in eleven seconds. Martha spends one minute, fourteen seconds. The result is the same: a mixture resembling coarse meal.

3. It's a good idea to keep a pitcher of ice water nearby. With the machine running, Sophie adds water gradually until the dough just holds together, in about eight seconds. She takes time out to help Aunt Martha measure her water.

4. Dough should still be a bit crumbly when done; overworked, it becomes gluey and tough.

5. Martha turns the dough out onto a sheet of plastic wrap, holding the food-processor blade in place from the bottom of the work bowl.

6. Martha and Sophie pat the dough into flat rounds, then wrap them in plastic to be chilled. These rounds will be easier to roll out than the traditional ball of dough.

7. Dough should be rolled on a lightly floured surface. Always roll from the center toward the edges—not back and forth—and pick up the pin before each stroke. Brush off excess flour, using a dry brush reserved for that purpose.

8. Sophie uses a pie tin as a guide to estimate her crust size, cutting at least an inch beyond the rim.

9. Martha shows Sophie how to line her pie tin: fold the circle in half, center it in the tin, and unfold it. To make sure it doesn't shrink when baked, they push the dough into the corners and gently in toward the center. Then the crust is refrigerated for thirty minutes.

10. Martha weaves a lattice on a sheet of baking parchment with strips she cut and chilled ahead of time. She folds back every other lengthwise strip, lays a crosswise strip, unfolds everything flat, then repeats the process with alternating strips until the weaving is complete.

11. Meanwhile, Sophie has prepared her apple slices. She piles them high in her crust, careful not to let any of them poke a hole in the dough.

12. To keep the crust from getting soggy, Sophie waits until the last minute to squeeze lemon juice over the apples, then dots the top with butter.

13. Sophie tops her pie with lattice and trims off the excess, pressing the side of the knife against the tin so as not to tug at the pastry.

14. Sophie crimps her pie, forming a scallop with her thumb and two fingers.

15. Martha brushes her pie with egg-and-cream glaze to give it a glossy finish when baked.

Apple pie lends itself to a variety of pastry treatments. On the page opposite, Martha and Sophie top theirs with a lattice of pâte brisée. THIS PAGE: A double-crust pie, with vents for steam, cools beside a free-form bottom-crust pie.

Maple Pecan Pie

SERVES 10 TO 12

We tend not to think of nuts in terms of freshness, but we should, for a stale nut can ruin a pie. If you can wheedle a supply of pecans from a friend with a tree, do so. If not, purchase whole nuts from a good supplier and chop them yourself.

1	recipe Pâte Brisée (see page 29)
3	large eggs
½	cup pure maple syrup
½	cup dark corn syrup
½	cup dark brown sugar
4	tablespoons (½ stick) unsalted butter, melted
1	teaspoon vanilla extract
	Grated zest of 1 lemon
1	teaspoon fresh lemon juice
1½	cups coarsely chopped pecans
1	cup perfect pecan halves
1	large egg beaten with 2 tablespoons heavy cream, for glaze
	Whipped cream (optional)

1. Roll out half the dough to a thickness of ⅛ inch and use to line a 9-inch pie tin, leaving a 1-inch overhang. Fold under evenly, indenting all around with your thumb. Roll out remaining dough and cut out four dozen leaves. Cut four ⅝-inch-wide strips a little longer than diameter of pie. Set on a parchment-lined baking sheet. Chill all pastry until firm.

2. Whisk together eggs, syrups, and brown sugar. Stir in melted butter, vanilla, lemon zest, and lemon juice. Fold in chopped pecans.

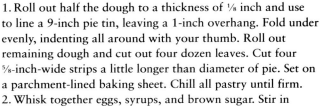

3. Pour filling into pie shell. Carefully apply pastry strips about an inch apart across top of pie, trimming off any overhang. Brush strips with ice water, and attach leaves end to end. Place a leaf on each thumbprint, attaching with ice water. Place pecan halves in spaces between strips (see left). Chill until firm.

4. Heat oven to 375°. Brush exposed pastry with egg glaze. Bake for 40 minutes, or until knife tip comes out clean. Serve warm or cold, with whipped cream if desired.

Pumpkin pie gets snaggle teeth made with a knife or scissors. We made the leaves on the maple-pecan pie with a Japanese cutter, but you could shape them freehand.

Pumpkin Pie

*Make sure your spices smell fresh before using them; they should
be replaced every year.*

½	recipe Pâte Brisée (see page 29)
1	small sugar pumpkin (about 3 pounds) or one 15-ounce can solid-pack pumpkin
4	large eggs
½	cup unsulfured molasses
¼	cup dark brown sugar
1	cup heavy cream
1	teaspoon cinnamon
½	teaspoon ground ginger
¼	teaspoon ground cloves
1	teaspoon salt
1	large egg beaten with 2 tablespoons heavy cream, for egg glaze

1. Roll out dough to a thickness of ⅛ inch and use to line
a 9-inch pie tin, leaving a 1½-inch overhang all around. Carefully fold under, making sure double edge is even. Gently
press to seal layers. Using a sharp paring knife or scissors,
cut V's all around. Fold alternating V's forward (see top pic-
ture, opposite page). Chill until firm, at least 30 minutes.
2. If using fresh pumpkin, cut into large chunks, removing
seeds and strings. Steam over boiling water in a heavy
saucepan for 25 to 30 minutes, until fork-tender. Drain
and let pumpkin cool slightly. Using a sharp spoon, scrape
cooked pumpkin from skin and put in bowl of a food
processor; puree. Measure out 1¾ cups puree (extra puree
can be refrigerated for use at a later date).
3. Heat oven to 375°. Combine puree and remaining filling
ingredients in a medium bowl and whisk until smooth. Brush
edges of crust with egg glaze. Pour filling into chilled pie shell
and bake for about 1 hour, or until edges are golden brown
and filling is set. Serve at room temperature.

**ABOVE RIGHT: Pumpkin pie, served in its old pie tin, with Bakelite-
handled forks. RIGHT: Maple-pecan pie with a dab of cream on white
ironstone plates; the forks are Georgian silver.**

For a crisp bottom crust to this classic piled-high lemon meringue pie, the shell was baked in the scalloped tin before filling. Setting the pie on a rack (this one is Victorian) to cool also helps prevent a soggy or doughy bottom.

Lemon Meringue Pie

SERVES 8 TO 10

This Swiss-meringue topping is light, and not too sweet.

½ recipe Pâte Brisée (see page 29)
1 large egg beaten with 2 tablespoons heavy cream,
   for egg glaze

FILLING

1¼ cups sugar
6   tablespoons cornstarch
2   cups water
½   cup fresh lemon juice
5   large egg yolks
    Pinch of salt
2   tablespoons grated lemon zest
4   tablespoons (½ stick) unsalted butter, cut into pieces

SWISS MERINGUE

7   large egg whites
¾   cup sugar
¼   teaspoon salt

1. Heat oven to 400°. Roll out dough to a thickness of ⅛ inch and use to line a 9-inch pie tin. Crimp edges decoratively. Chill until firm. Prick bottom of shell with a fork, brush edges with egg glaze, and line with aluminum foil. Weight with pie weights or beans. Bake until edges begin to turn brown, 10 to 15 minutes. Remove foil and weights; continue baking until golden brown, 7 to 10 minutes more. Let cool.
2. To make filling, sift together sugar and cornstarch in a small bowl. Stir in water until mixture is smooth.
3. In a nonreactive saucepan over medium heat, combine lemon juice, egg yolks, and salt. Stir in cornstarch mixture. Cook, stirring constantly, until mixture comes to a boil. Lower heat and cook until mixture falls off spoon in thick clumps, 2 to 3 minutes. Remove from heat; stir in zest and butter until smooth. Pour into a bowl; let cool to room temperature, stirring occasionally.
4. Pour filling into cooled pie shell and refrigerate, covered, until firm, about 1 hour.
5. To make meringue, combine egg whites, sugar, and salt in a heatproof bowl set over simmering water. Beat until sugar is dissolved. Remove from heat; whip until stiff peaks form.
6. Heat broiler. Spread meringue over pie so that it covers filling and touches crust all around. Broil until brown, watching constantly. Serve at room temperature.

PIE COLLECTING

The pie is such a ubiquitous dish, it's natural that a whole culture of implements should have been invented to accompany it. Pie servers, like these Victorian examples from America and England, with their sterling, mother-of-pearl, and ivory handles, are the least of it. There are pie racks, pie plates, pie chimneys (for venting steam), and pie tins. Until midway through this century, bakeries sold pies in metal tins that were returned for a ten-cent deposit (except in New Haven, where Yale students kept Mrs. Frisbee's tins to throw in the game that bears her name).

Pear Dumplings

MAKES 8

The poached pears must be prepared at least six hours before you assemble the dumplings; it's easiest to make them the day before.

1	recipe Pâte Brisée (see page 29)
½	cup sugar
4	teaspoons cinnamon
8	Poached Pears, chilled and drained (recipe follows)
4	tablespoons (½ stick) cold butter, cut into small pieces
1	large egg beaten with 2 tablespoons heavy cream, for egg glaze

1. Roll out pastry to a thickness of ⅛ inch. Cut out eight squares measuring approximately 8 by 8 inches. Cut a triangle with roughly equal sides from each square and set aside. Cut as many leaves as possible out of the remaining pastry either by hand with a sharp knife or with a leaf-shaped cutter. Keep all pastry covered and chilled until ready to use.
2. Mix sugar and cinnamon together in a small bowl. Core each poached pear carefully from the bottom to just within ¾ inch of top; leave stem intact. Holding pear upside down, fill with some of the sugar mixture and dots of butter. Place center of pastry triangle on pear bottom, then turn so pear is right side up. Bring edges together, moisten with water, and pinch to seal. Decorate dumplings as desired by pasting leaves on with water (see left). Keep stems free of pastry. Place on a parchment-lined baking sheet and chill if pastry has softened.
3. Heat oven to 400°. Lightly brush each dumpling with egg glaze and bake until puffed and golden brown, 20 to 25 minutes. Let cool on a wire rack for at least 15 minutes. Serve warm or at room temperature.

Poached Pears

MAKES 8

The pears can be served on their own as a light dessert or used in pies and dumplings.

½	vanilla bean, split and scraped
1	bottle champagne, sparkling white wine, or dry white wine
2	tablespoons fresh lemon juice
1	cup sugar
1	cinnamon stick
	Zest of 1 lemon
8	firm but ripe Bartlett pears, peeled

The pears for these dumplings must be poached with their stems left on to serve as handles. Left to cool overnight, the poached pears become firm, thus easier to wrap in their pâte brisée crusts.

1. In a large saucepan over medium heat, combine vanilla bean and scrapings with rest of ingredients except pears. Bring mixture to a boil and cook for 5 minutes.

2. Add pears, lower heat, and cover with a pot lid slightly smaller than pan to keep pears submerged. Cook until tender, 20 to 30 minutes. If necessary, turn pears gently so they cook evenly.

3. Transfer pears and liquid to a bowl, and refrigerate, covered, for at least 6 hours, preferably overnight.

Pear Pie in Cornmeal Crust

SERVES 8 TO 10

This recipe resembles a cross between a European tart and an American pie. Poach the pears the day before you make the pie.

1	bottle dry red wine
1	cup sugar
4	whole cloves
2-3	cinnamon sticks
10	ripe but firm Bartlett or Anjou pears, peeled, cored, and cut into 1-inch cubes
1	recipe Cornmeal Pastry (recipe follows)
1	tablespoon all-purpose flour
1	large egg beaten with 2 tablespoons heavy cream, for egg glaze

1. Combine wine, sugar, cloves, and cinnamon sticks in a large saucepan. Bring to a boil over medium heat. Lower heat and simmer until liquid is reduced by a third, 10 to 15 minutes. Add pears and poach at a bare simmer until tender, 15 to 30 minutes, depending on ripeness. Keep pears submerged with a pot lid slightly smaller than pan.

2. Remove pears to a large bowl using a slotted spoon. Reduce liquid by half over high heat. Pour over pears and let cool to room temperature; refrigerate, covered, overnight.

3. Prepare Cornmeal Pastry as directed. Roll out the dough to a thickness of ⅛ inch and use to line a 9-inch pie tin. Chill until needed. Roll out remaining dough to a thickness of ⅛ inch and a diameter of 11 inches. Transfer to a parchment-lined baking sheet and cover; chill for 30 minutes.

4. Heat oven to 375°. Sprinkle tablespoon of flour over bottom of chilled piecrust. Remove spices from poaching liquid and discard. Remove pears with a slotted spoon and

ABOVE RIGHT: Pear pie in cornmeal crust is served with a slice of Gorgonzola cheese and a sprig of lavender on an octagonal French plate. RIGHT: Pear dumplings on a filigreed silver tray.

place in crust. (Don't worry if a little of the poaching liquid ends up in the pie.)

5. Let top crust sit at room temperature for a few minutes before attempting to move it. Brush edges of bottom crust lightly with ice water. Carefully cover pears with top crust and crimp edges, sealing well. Cut a few small steam vents near center, and lightly brush top crust with egg glaze. Bake until top is golden brown and juices start to bubble out, 50 to 60 minutes. Let cool for 1 hour.

CORNMEAL PASTRY

MAKES TWO 9-INCH CRUSTS

1½	cups all-purpose flour
½	cup yellow cornmeal
½	cup sugar
1	teaspoon salt
8	tablespoons (1 stick) cold unsalted butter, cut into small pieces
2	large egg yolks
3-4	tablespoons ice water

1. In a large bowl, mix together flour, cornmeal, sugar, and salt. Rub in butter with your fingers until crumbly.
2. Mix together egg yolks and ice water in a small bowl. Mix into dry ingredients, stirring with a fork. Knead lightly in the bowl until dough holds together; add more water if it seems dry. Divide dough in half and press into two flat disks; wrap in plastic. Chill until firm, about 30 minutes.
NOTE: This dough is more crumbly than pâte brisée; roll out dough between two sheets of plastic wrap.

ANTIQUE APPLES

We make pies from all sorts of fruits, from nuts, even from vegetables. But the classic American pie is apple, made from several varieties of the fruit for depth of flavor. The local supermarket is unlikely to carry a large selection: eighty percent of the U.S. apple production is now limited to just eight varieties, bred more for sturdiness than for taste. To taste a real range of apples, visit one of the orchards where old varieties thrive.

At Breezy Hill Orchard in New York State, the thirty-five varieties of apple tree planted in 1949 are still fruitful. The current owners sell the full array at the Union Square farmers' market in New York City, and find that "many people have never really had a good, flavorful, crisp apple right off the tree."

Those who have tasted an old-fashioned apple fresh from the tree may wish to start a home orchard. Since most apple trees require cross-pollination to reproduce, the orchard will need at least two varieties that flower at about the same time. They must be planted as far apart as they will grow tall; standard trees grow to thirty feet, so home gardeners should concentrate on dwarf and semi-dwarf varieties. This won't limit the selection; any variety can be grafted onto dwarfing rootstock.

Early autumn morning at Breezy Hill Orchard in New York's Hudson River Valley. OPPOSITE: Stayman Winesaps, ripe for eating.

Apple growing and picking is hard physical work. Breezy Hill's owners are rewarded when customers at New York City's Union Square farmers' market—who once dismissed apples as "boring"—return often to trade notes on favorite varieties.

OUR FAVORITE BAKING APPLES

AKANE: Relatively new entry from Japan. Bright-red fruit; crisp flavor reminiscent of underripe strawberries.

ARKANSAS BLACK: Small, purplish-red apple with fine-grained, yellowish flesh. High acid content, sprightly flavor, and hard texture.

BALDWIN: Green blushed with bright red, occasionally flecked with russet. Crisp, aromatic, agreeably acidic flesh.

BURGUNDY: Large fruit with a smooth blackish-red skin. Its juicy, winey flesh tends to break down in cooking.

CORTLAND: Red with green highlights; tart yet tender flavors may bear hints of butterscotch; good for salads, too.

COX'S ORANGE PIPPIN: Old English favorite with thin, smooth skin washed an appealing orange-red. Juicy, crisp flesh has spicy notes.

ELSTAR: Bright shades of yellow, orange, and red; sweet-tart flavors; good for snacks, salads, baking.

EMPIRE: Dark red with tart juiciness; good all-purpose apple.

GOLDEN DELICIOUS: Yellow, sometimes flushed with pale orange; crisp, juicy, sweetly aromatic; occasionally musky, mellow. Keeps shape well in cooking.

GOLDEN RUSSET: Thick-skinned, russet verging on bronze in color. Fine-grained, yellowish flesh is crisp, juicy, acidic; excellent all-purpose apple.

GRANNY SMITH: Grass-green; juicy, firm flesh noted for tartness; fruit holds shape, lends acid in cooking.

GRAVENSTEIN: Pale yellow with bands of orange-red; tangy-sweet flavors; crisp, juicy flesh.

IDARED: Greenish yellow flushed with crimson. Sweet, slightly watery flavor.

JONAGOLD: A cross between Golden Delicious and Jonathan; ripe yellow blushed with bright red; sweet with slight acidity and rich flavor. Good for snacking and desserts.

JONATHAN: Bright-yellow skin overlaid with lively red stripes; whitish flesh; juicy, highly aromatic; pronounced sweetness with balancing acidity.

LADY: Also called Pomme d'Apis. Small, oblong fruit with glossy red blush against whitish ground. Fine grained, crisp, acidic but also sweet.

MACOUN: High sugars with balancing acidity make this apple good for desserts where a soft texture is desired.

MUTSU: Yellowish green sometimes flushed with grayed orange; fairly sweet-tart for snacking; consistent and firm for cooking. A Japanese apple marketed in some areas as Crispin.

NORTHERN SPY: Large; green background overlaid with muted red. Crisp flesh with a sweet-tart complexity and robust flavor; outstanding for cooking.

RHODE ISLAND GREENING: Ideal for cooking and dessert. Large; grass-green ripening to richer yellow; tart but tender and juicy.

ROME BEAUTY: Glossy red skin; firm, white flesh with tart flavor.

ROXBURY RUSSET: Greenish to yellowish brown russeted skin; sweet flesh suitable for dessert and cider.

ROYAL GALA: Firm, yellowish flesh with deep-orange stripes; sweet aroma and flavor; good dessert apple.

SNOW APPLE or **FAMEUSE:** Bright red verging on purple on a green background; solid, very white flesh with rich, aromatic, slightly sweet flavor.

STAYMAN WINESAP: Large; rough, purplish-red skin; tastes like cherries; a favorite for snacking, cooking, and cider.

WINTER BANANA: Clear, pale yellow with pinkish-red blush. Yellow-tinged white flesh; tender and very mild.

YORK IMPERIAL: Deep red, sometimes striped green; enticing, musky flavors. Good for processing, pies, and sauces.

Homemade Gifts

IF, AS THEY SAY, IT IS THE THOUGHT THAT COUNTS rather than the gift, then a homemade gift is doubly welcome. We like to give careful consideration to the tastes and pastimes of the recipient, then to spend time making a gift from the kitchen or garden—or, at times, the tag sale. We know a gift will be successful when we covet it for ourselves, which happens so often we tend to make duplicates when possible. At a time when the holidays can seem overly commercial, it is a joy to see what pleasure comes from a simple, inexpensive, but beautiful present made by the hand and heart.

Citrus Shortbread

MAKES ABOUT 18 COOKIES

We prepared three batches of shortbread using a different zest in each, then cut each kind into a different shape.

½	pound (2 sticks) unsalted butter, slightly softened
⅔	cup sifted confectioners' sugar
1	tablespoon grated orange, lemon, or lime zest
1	teaspoon pure orange, lemon, or lime extract
2	cups sifted all-purpose flour
¼	teaspoon salt

1. Using an electric mixer fitted with the paddle attachment, cream butter until fluffy. Beat in sugar, zest, and matching extract.
2. Combine flour and salt and mix into butter mixture on low speed just until combined. Do not overmix.
3. Knead a few times on a lightly floured board and roll out to a thickness of ¼ inch. Cut into desired shapes with well-floured cookie cutters and transfer to a parchment-lined baking sheet. Prick each cookie with a fork a few times and chill until firm, about 30 minutes.
4. Heat oven to 350°. Bake shortbread for about 20 minutes, or until it just begins to brown. Cool completely on a rack. Shortbread will keep for a few weeks in an airtight container.

OPPOSITE: As recently as the 1940s, many children tasted fresh citrus only when a Christmas stocking held an orange in the toe. We keep the tradition, tucking a tissue-wrapped Valencia into gift baskets. THIS PAGE: Four flavors of citrus shortbread in a Shaker box.

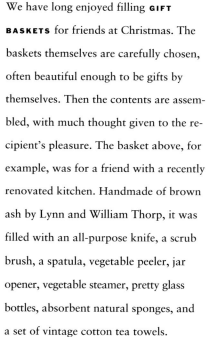

We have long enjoyed filling **GIFT BASKETS** for friends at Christmas. The baskets themselves are carefully chosen, often beautiful enough to be gifts by themselves. Then the contents are assembled, with much thought given to the recipient's pleasure. The basket above, for example, was for a friend with a recently renovated kitchen. Handmade of brown ash by Lynn and William Thorp, it was filled with an all-purpose knife, a scrub brush, a spatula, vegetable peeler, jar opener, vegetable steamer, pretty glass bottles, absorbent natural sponges, and a set of vintage cotton tea towels.

Almost any heatproof and leakproof container can be made into a **CANDLE**. We have used eggcups, small flowerpots (with the drainage holes taped over), and shells, like the big, fluted clamshells, above. First nestle the empty shells into supporting cups of crumpled aluminum foil. Coil wicking in centers; tape ends of wicks to support above shells so wicks are upright. Melt beeswax in a heatproof but disposable container and carefully spoon into shells, centering wicks as wax nears top. When wax has hardened, trim wicks. Pack carefully, surrounding shells with plenty of crumpled paper.

The **GIFT FOR A TEA LOVER:** we found this buttercup-yellow vintage Spode tea set at a tag sale. Padded with lots and lots of colorful tissue paper, it was accompanied by a sterling tea ball from Tiffany's, vintage sterling teaspoons, yellow rock-crystal sugar, French brown-sugar cubes, and a tin of good, strong tea from Fortnum and Mason. We have made companion baskets for coffee drinkers, filled with huge café-au-lait bowls, good beans, a coffee grinder, a plunger pot (or a gold-plated mesh filter for a drip coffee machine), and a bag of freshly baked hazelnut biscotti.

FLAVORED OILS AND VINEGARS make a welcome gift for a cook. Buy decorative new containers, or reuse old bottles. (To clean, put in two tablespoons of uncooked rice, add hot soapy water, and shake vigorously.) Wash and dry herbs, and place three or four generous sprigs in each bottle. Using a funnel, fill bottles with oils or vinegars until herbs are completely submerged. We have used hot peppers, rosemary, tarragon, thyme, sage, dill, and black peppercorns. Garlic is delicious, but should be added only to vinegars, not oil. Cork or seal bottles; they'll be ready to use in three weeks.

Plain white **NAPKINS AND TABLECLOTHS** can be personalized for friends with fabric paint. Choose natural fabrics—linen or cotton are best. Wash to remove sizing; when dry, pin fabric flat to board to provide a stable work surface. We outlined napkins with copper paint. Oil-based paints, including most metallics, will harden when dry, so should not be used in the center of a napkin. We have also painted linens (including pillowcases) with washable water-based fabric paint, which dries more softly. Huge initials, stylized shells and flowers, and numbers have turned simple fabrics into gifts.

Virgil is one of our favorite friends, and deserves a **PET'S BASKET** to himself. We provided a bed of cedar shavings enclosed in a claw-proof removable (and washable) cover, a red Boomer Ball, a clear plastic flying disk and bone, a rope tug toy, a leather collar and leash, wide-bottomed one and two quart bowls designed so they can't be turned over by the hungriest puppy, a string of doggy bagels, a rawhide bone, assorted treats, and a book to help his mistress keep him in line. We have made similar gifts for cats, with plenty of catnip toys in a cushioned basket that becomes a bed itself.

Three Fruit Marmalade

MAKES FIVE 8-OUNCE JARS

*This marmalade is more like a jelly with some shreds of peel.
Cut the peel thick or thin, as you like it.*

1   grapefruit
1   orange
2   lemons
2   quarts water
6¾   cups sugar

1. Scrub fruit, place in a large bowl, and cover with boiling water. Let stand 2 minutes, then drain. Remove peel in thin slices with a zester, or cut off with a sharp knife into thicker pieces, as desired. Tie peel in a piece of cheesecloth; set aside.
2. Chop remaining pith and fruit into small pieces. You can do this with a food processor, but do not puree.
3. Combine chopped fruit, cheesecloth bag, and water in a 4-quart stainless-steel pan. Cover and simmer 1½ hours over low heat, until reduced by almost half. Remove cheesecloth bag and set aside.
4. Strain contents of pan, pressing to extract liquid. Discard solids and return liquid to pan. Add sugar and dissolve over low heat. Bring to a boil. Add peel from cheesecloth and simmer over medium heat 10 to 30 minutes, until mixture reaches 221° on a candy thermometer or falls in sheets from a spoon.
5. Pour into sterilized jars, seal, and cool.
LIME MARMALADE VARIATION: Substitute 9 limes for the grapefruit, orange, and lemons. Use the peel from 4 of the limes in the cheesecloth in step 1. Add the juice of 2 lemons with the fruit in step 3.

LEFT: Homemade citrus preserves—spicy orange relish and marmalades made from limes, oranges, and blood oranges—are poured into sterilized jars, sealed, and topped with photocopies of old citrus prints and ribbon ties.

Spiced Oranges

MAKES 2 QUARTS

Serve these sweet-sour oranges like a chutney.

9   Valencia or blood oranges, scrubbed and sliced
      ¼-inch thick
4   cups sugar
2   cups white-wine vinegar
2   cinnamon sticks
10   whole cloves
15   black peppercorns

1. Place orange slices in a stainless-steel saucepan; cover with cold water. Simmer until skins are tender, about 1¼ hours.
2. Remove oranges with a slotted spoon; place in a colander to drain. Discard water.
3. Combine sugar and vinegar in the same saucepan; stir over low heat. Bring to a boil. Add spices; simmer 10 minutes.
4. Add oranges and simmer, covered, for 40 minutes, or until skins are translucent. Cool.
5. Layer oranges in sterilized jars, cover with syrup, and seal. The oranges can be used right away, but the flavor will be improved by waiting 4 to 6 weeks.

Blood Orange Marmalade

MAKES THREE 8-OUNCE JARS

Other types of oranges can be substituted to make this chunky marmalade, but it won't have the same pink hue.

3   blood oranges
4   cups water
      Zest and juice of 2 lemons
3-4   cups sugar, as needed

1. Scrub oranges. Cut in half lengthwise and slice as thinly as possible. Cut slices into eighths, reserving all juice. In a medium bowl, combine slices with water and zest, cover, and let stand at least 12 hours.
2. Transfer mixture to a large stainless-steel saucepan over medium heat; bring to a boil. Simmer 30 minutes; add lemon juice.
3. Measure total volume of fruit and liquid and add ¾ cup sugar for every cup. Stir to dissolve and bring to a boil over high heat. Boil 30 to 60 minutes, until mixture reaches 221° on a candy thermometer or falls in sheets from a spoon.
4. Pour into sterilized jars, seal, and cool.

Afternoon Tea

FOR ALL ITS FOPPISH CONNOTATIONS, AFTERNOON tea is a splendidly practical meal—especially for holiday entertaining. All the dishes (save the tea itself, of course) can be made in advance, the number of guests can be extremely flexible, and the table or tray can be set with grace in almost any location. After all, Anna, the seventh Duchess of Bedford, who invented the ritual of afternoon tea, gave her well-attended parties in the bedroom. We are not quite that casual, but we like to give afternoon teas in the garden, the library, the kitchen, as well as the parlor proper. We serve plates of crumpets, tartlets, sandwiches, and cakes, but we do not forget the centerpiece, the pot of tea. Our favorite is Rose Pouchong, which friends bring from London's Fortnum and Mason.

MENU

Pear and Stilton Tartlets

Orange Madeleines

Apple Rosemary Tea Bread

Molasses Ginger Scones

Currant Scones

Poppy-Seed Cake

Crumpets

Neapolitan Sandwiches

LEFT: **Early English teapots were silver; as tea trickled down the classes, pottery was popular.** RIGHT: **Catskill Moss tea bowl and saucer.**

PHOTOGRAPHS BY JOHN DUGDALE

GROWING TEA

Camellia sinensis is an evergreen that grows best in the semitropics.

During its growing season, the two top leaves and bud of the

three-foot-high tea bush are harvested every fifteen to eighteen days.

The tea is placed in troughs to wither, then ground and allowed to oxidize,

and finally dried or "fired" until it turns the familiar black.

Pear and Stilton Tartlets

MAKES 16 TARTLETS

The whole-wheat tartlet shells can be made a day in advance, stored in an airtight tin, and filled with their slices of pear and Stilton just before serving.

WHOLE WHEAT PASTRY

¾   cup whole-wheat flour
1¾ cup all-purpose flour
1   teaspoon salt
8   tablespoons (1 stick) butter, chilled
½   cup vegetable shortening, chilled
½   cup ice water

1. To make pastry, thoroughly combine flours and salt in a medium bowl. Cut in butter and shortening with a pastry blender until mixture resembles coarse meal.
2. Drizzle ice water into mixture while stirring with a fork. As soon as pastry holds together when squeezed, stop adding water. Form dough into a ball, wrap in plastic, and chill at least 1 hour.
3. Roll out dough to ⅛ inch thick and line small barquette molds or other small tartlet shells with pastry. Prick bottoms with a fork and chill for 30 minutes. Wrap leftover dough in plastic and store in freezer for later use.
4. Line tartlets with foil, leaving edges of pastry exposed. Re-chill until firm if necessary.
5. Heat oven to 375°. Bake shells for about 8 minutes, or until pastry looks dry and set on the bottom. Remove foil and bake 4 minutes longer, or until lightly browned. Let cool.

FILLING

1   pear, preferably Seckel, thinly sliced
    Watercress
2   ounces Stilton, crumbled

When ready to serve, fill each tartlet shell with a thin slice of pear, a watercress leaf, and crumbled Stilton.

OPPOSITE: Madeleines on a transfer-printed plate made in America in the 1870s. TOP LEFT: Apple rosemary bread on old English china. LEFT: Pear and Stilton tartlets arranged on a glass cake stand.

Orange Madeleines

MAKES 36

It's worth finding proper shell-shape madeleine molds for this recipe; they're useful for making decorative shortbreads, too.

8	tablespoons (1 stick) unsalted butter
4	large eggs
¼	teaspoon salt
⅔	cup sugar
½	teaspoon vanilla extract
½	teaspoon orange-flower water
1	cup sifted all-purpose flour
1	teaspoon grated orange zest
	Confectioners' sugar, for dusting tops

1. Butter and flour madeleine molds thoroughly. Set aside. Heat oven to 350°.
2. Melt butter and let cool.
3. Beat together eggs, salt, and sugar until very fluffy. Beat in vanilla and orange-flower water. Fold in flour, then the melted butter and orange zest.
4. Pour batter into molds almost to the top. Bake for 10 minutes, or until cakes are firm in the center. Let cool for 1 minute in molds, then turn out onto racks. Dust tops with confectioners' sugar before serving.

Apple Rosemary Tea Bread

MAKES 3 SMALL LOAVES

Drizzle slices of this aromatic bread with warm clover honey.

¾	cup plus 1 tablespoon milk
½	cup raisins, coarsely chopped
4	tablespoons (½ stick) plus 1 teaspoon unsalted butter
2	apples, peeled, cored, and diced
½	cup plus 1 tablespoon sugar
1	teaspoon chopped rosemary
1½	cups all-purpose flour
2	teaspoons baking powder
¼	teaspoon salt
1	large egg

1. Heat oven to 350°. Butter and flour three 5½-by-2½-by-2-inch loaf pans. Set them aside.
2. Heat milk to scalding. Remove from heat and add raisins. Stir in 4 tablespoons of the butter and let cool.
3. In a small sauté pan over medium heat, cook apples in remaining 1 teaspoon butter with the 1 tablespoon sugar until apples are glazed and somewhat soft, about 3 minutes. Add rosemary.
4. Combine flour, remaining ½ cup sugar, baking powder, and salt. Whisk the egg into cooled milk-raisin mixture.
5. Add the diced apples to dry ingredients but don't combine. Pour wet mixture over the dry and mix with a few quick strokes, until dry ingredients are just moistened. Do not overmix.
6. Fill prepared pans to about ¾ full. Bake for 20 minutes, or until a toothpick inserted into middle comes out clean. Let cool.

ACCOUTREMENTS OF TEA

There is no excuse for the tea bag. It takes no more time or effort to toss spoonfuls of loose tea into a pot; the only investment is a small strainer to keep floating leaves out of the cup. To make a single cup, a tea ball or infuser can be used. Below: Caddy spoons for measuring tea, strainers, a tea ball, and "mote spoons" to capture leaves that escape the strainer.

ABOVE: Like oriental tea bowls, the oldest American and English teacups are without handles. **OPPOSITE:** When they emerge from the oven, scones should be wrapped in a napkin to keep them soft and warm. Serve with raspberry jam and clotted cream.

Molasses Ginger Scones

MAKES 10 TO 12

These rich, spicy scones are delicious plain, but for a real treat, serve them with a bit of jam or lemon curd (see page 57).

2	cups all-purpose flour
2	tablespoons sugar, plus additional for garnish
1	tablespoon baking powder
½	teaspoon ground ginger
	Pinch of salt
8	tablespoons (1 stick) unsalted butter, chilled
2	ounces candied ginger, chopped
1	large egg
3	tablespoons unsulfured molasses
¼	cup heavy cream
1	beaten egg, for wash

1. Heat oven to 400°. Lightly butter a baking sheet and set aside.
2. Twice sift together flour, sugar, baking powder, ground ginger, and salt. Cut in butter by hand or with a pastry blender until mixture resembles coarse meal. Stir in chopped candied ginger.
3. Beat together egg, molasses, and cream. Make a well in the center of dry ingredients and pour in egg mixture. Stir lightly with a fork just until dough comes together. Turn out onto a lightly floured surface and knead a few times to mix well, but do not overwork dough.
4. Pat dough into a rectangle or circle about ¾ inch thick. Cut into 2½-inch triangles with a floured knife or into shapes with floured cookie cutters.
5. Transfer scones to prepared baking sheet. Brush tops with beaten egg and sprinkle with sugar. Bake 12 to 15 minutes, or until an even golden brown. Cool on wire racks.

Currant Scones

MAKES 10 TO 12

If not eaten warm from the oven, scones are best split, toasted, and spread with butter or clotted cream and jam.

2	cups all-purpose flour
1	tablespoon baking powder
3	tablespoons sugar, plus additional for tops
½	teaspoon salt
6	tablespoons (¾ stick) unsalted butter, chilled
½	cup dried currants
2	large eggs
⅓	cup heavy cream
1	beaten egg, for wash

1. Heat oven to 400°. Lightly butter a baking sheet and set aside.
2. Twice sift together flour, baking powder, sugar, and salt. Cut in butter with a pastry blender until mixture resembles coarse meal. Stir in currants.
3. Beat together eggs and cream. Make a well in center of dry ingredients and pour in egg mixture. Stir lightly with a fork just until dough comes together. Turn out onto a slightly floured surface and knead a few times to mix well.
4. Pat dough into a rectangle or circle until ¾ inch thick. Cut into 2½-inch triangles with a floured knife or into shapes with floured cookie cutters.
5. Transfer scones to prepared baking sheet. Brush tops with beaten egg and sprinkle with sugar. Bake 12 to 15 minutes, or until an even, golden brown. Cool on wire racks.

The Victorian love of excess is reflected in their teapots, especially silver lusterware, or "poor man's silver." These ceramic pots glazed with silver offered a little bit of luxury to those of modest means. A luscious poppy seed cake, filled and frosted with lemon curd, would have satisfied the Victorian sweet tooth.

Poppy Seed Cake

SERVES 10 TO 12

The recipe for this rich, classic tea cake may seem daunting, but you can bake and assemble the cake the day before serving.

1	cup milk
½	cup poppy seeds, plus additional for garnish
	Grated zest of 1 lemon
1	tablespoon vanilla extract
2½	cups all-purpose flour, sifted before measuring
1	tablespoon baking powder
	Pinch of salt
½	pound (2 sticks) unsalted butter, softened
1½	cups sugar
4	large eggs, at room temperature
2	cups Lemon Curd (recipe follows)
1	cup (½ pint) heavy cream
	Long strips of lemon zest, for garnish

1. Heat oven to 350°. Butter two 8-inch round cake pans. Line bottoms with parchment paper, then butter and flour the paper and sides of pans. Set aside.

2. In a small saucepan over high heat, combine milk, poppy seeds, and lemon zest. Heat to scalding, then allow to cool to room temperature. Add vanilla.

3. Twice sift together flour, baking powder, and salt. Set aside.

4. Using an electric mixer fitted with the paddle attachment, cream butter at low speed until fluffy, about 2 minutes. Gradually add sugar and beat on medium speed until very fluffy, about 5 minutes. Scrape down sides several times during mixing.

5. Add eggs one at a time, beating well after each addition. Beat on medium high speed until smooth, about 1 minute.

6. Blend in the flour mixture in 3 additions and milk mixture in 2 additions, beginning and ending with flour. Beat on low speed only until mixed. The mixing process should take less than 2 minutes.

7. Divide batter evenly between prepared pans and bake 25 to 30 minutes, or until a toothpick inserted in the middle of the cakes comes out clean. Let cool in pans 5 minutes, then turn out onto wire racks. Peel off paper and cool completely.

8. To assemble cake, place one of the layers on a serving plate. Spread on about 1 cup of chilled Lemon Curd to within ¾ inch of edge. Place second layer right side up on filling and press gently. Chill for 30 minutes.

9. Whip cream until it holds soft peaks. Fold into remaining cup of Lemon Curd. Keep cold over a bowl of ice water.

10. Quickly ice top and sides of cake with a thick layer of cream-curd mixture, trying to cover most of the cake. Chill for 15 to 30 minutes. Ice cake again to cover completely. Chill to set, about 15 minutes.

11. Tipping cake slightly, sprinkle sides with poppy seeds. Decorate top with long strips of lemon zest. Chill until ready to serve.

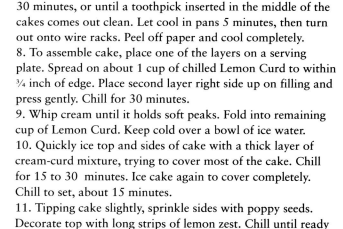

Long, slender curls of citrus peel are easy to produce with a citrus zester, and can be used to decorate cookies, cut fruits (orange peel complements strawberries), or cakes. We edged our poppy seed cake, filled and iced with lemon curd, with lemon peel.

Lemon Curd

MAKES ABOUT 3 CUPS

Lemon curd is a tangy topping for scones and crumpets.

1   cup sugar
6   egg yolks, beaten and strained
½   cup fresh lemon juice, lightly beaten and strained
8   tablespoons (1 stick) unsalted butter, cut up
     Grated zest of 1 lemon

1. Place sugar, egg yolks, and lemon juice in a medium saucepan over low heat. Whisk to combine, then switch to a wooden spoon. Cook slowly, stirring constantly, until mixture thickens and coats the back of the spoon. Cook a few minutes more but do not allow to boil.
2. Remove from heat, stir in butter and zest, and let cool. Cover with plastic wrap and chill until ready to use.

Crumpets

MAKES 16

If you don't have metal baking rings, clean tuna cans with the tops and bottoms removed make a fine substitute.

2¼   cups all-purpose flour
1   tablespoon active dry yeast
½   teaspoon sugar
1⅓   cups warm water
¾   cup milk
½   teaspoon baking soda
1   teaspoon salt

1. Sift half the flour into a large bowl. Add yeast, sugar, and water and blend until smooth. Let sit in a warm place until foamy, about 20 minutes.
2. Add ½ cup of the milk, the baking soda, salt, and remaining flour to the yeast mixture. Beat well, adding more milk if needed to make a thick batter of pouring consistency.
3. Oil a griddle or iron skillet and six metal baking rings. Thoroughly heat rings in the skillet over medium heat.
4. Pour 3 tablespoons of batter into each ring and cook for about 10 minutes, until the top looks set and holes appear. Remove rings from griddle, turn over crumpets, and cook 10 minutes more. Repeat until batter is used up. Serve immediately, or split and serve toasted.
NOTE: This recipe is from *The Afternoon Tea Book,* by Michael Smith.

The humble crumpet, drenched in butter and served with apricot preserves, is as timeless as Brownfield's English ironstone transferware from the 1870s.

Neapolitan Sandwiches

Don't overfill the layers or they will fall apart when you slice them. Each four-layer stack will make about ten small sandwiches.

Herbed Cream Cheese (recipe follows)
Thin-sliced whole-wheat and white breads
Cucumbers, preferably seedless, thinly sliced
Unsalted butter, softened
Radishes, thinly sliced
Watercress, large stems removed
Chopped fresh parsley

1. Spread cream cheese on a slice of whole-wheat bread and top with slightly overlapping slices of cucumber. (This will be the bottom layer of the sandwich.)
2. Spread cream cheese on a slice of white bread. Place on top of whole-wheat slice so that bare side faces up. Spread bare side of white-bread slice with butter and radish slices.
3. Top radishes with another slice of wheat bread spread with butter, bare side up. Spread the bare side of the wheat bread with cream cheese and watercress leaves.
4. Top the watercress leaves with white bread spread with cream cheese on one side. (The bare side will be the top layer of the sandwich.) Press down gently and chill until set, about 15 minutes. Trim off crusts and cut through all layers into thin slices. Dip edges in chopped fresh parsley if desired.

HERBED CREAM CHEESE

MAKES ABOUT 1 CUP

1   tablespoon chopped fresh chives
1   tablespoon chopped fresh parsley
1   tablespoon chopped fresh tarragon
8   ounces cream cheese, softened
     Salt and freshly ground pepper

Chop herbs by hand and fold into cream cheese by hand or with an electric mixer, adding salt and pepper to taste.

In the late eighteenth century, the French invented the "trembleuse" saucer, which has a recess so the cup won't slide. It was promptly adopted by British and American potters, who produced these teacups and saucers in the early nineteenth century.

BREWING TEA

Let the faucet run until the water is cold, fill the kettle and put to boil immediately. When the water reaches a rolling boil, pour a little into the teapot and swirl around to warm it. Empty the pot, then put in about one teaspoon of fresh, loose tea for each cup. Pour the water onto the tea, never vice versa. (And don't let the water boil too long, or you'll boil out too much oxygen.) Brew by the clock, three to five minutes, depending on taste. Never judge tea by its color, for each variety or blend brews to a different shade. Pour tea into cups through a tea strainer, and add thinly sliced lemon or milk, and sugar if desired. Don't try to pour yourself a second cup from a pot that has steeped for even a quarter of an hour; make a second pot instead.

ABOVE: Tea sandwiches. Clockwise from bottom left: butter and radish; cucumber with cream cheese; smoked salmon and dill; ham and apricot preserves; our "Neapolitans." RIGHT: Caddy, the word for a tea canister, comes from *kati*, a Malayan measure.

Gift Wrappings

THE PRESENTATION OF OUR GIFTS IS TREMENDOUSLY *important. The much desired but all too pragmatic present, the token for an unexpected guest, all become fantastic when wrapped in layers of shiny paper, tied with great, wide ribbons, and stacked beneath the tree. Store-bought wrapping paper and trims, however, are extremely expensive and somewhat impersonal. We prefer to make our own, using ordinary materials (shelf paper, Kraft paper, tissue, leaves, and berries) and painting or trimming them to match the color and theme of tree and house decorations. Parsimonious by nature, we also tend to save our wrappings, keeping boxes of carefully flattened papers tucked beneath the bed for use next year: The earth can do without another load of Christmas rubbish, so do recycle.*

OPPOSITE AND ABOVE: Homemade wrapping paper has both elegance and charm. Anticipation is part of the pleasure of giving, and getting: the perfect wrapping enhances the moment.

PAINTED PAPER

Much of our wrapping paper was made
from plain Kraft wrap, the sturdy brown
paper commonly used to protect packages
for mailing. We sponged, spattered, and
painted it with oil-based paints to luxurious effect.

Choose a well-ventilated work space:
oil paints, especially metallics, can be
toxic. Cover the work surface (we prefer
the floor) with sheets of plastic, then with
newspaper. Wearing latex gloves, stir
paints and pour into disposable foil or
plastic containers.

To produce the checkerboard effect
at left, you'll need a one-inch-wide bristle
brush and a steady hand. Start at the
upper corner of the paper, and daub with
a quick brushstroke across. Follow with
the next row.

Sponged patterns (see right) are produced with a piece of natural sea sponge
(natural rather than cellulose because the
irregular holes will make a prettier pattern). Tear a piece off the sponge, dampen
to soften, and dip into the paint. Dab
paint from sponge all over the paper in
rows or a random pattern as you desire.
Follow with a second color, if desired:
We found that two metallics—gold and
copper, for example—were very attractive.

Allow paint to dry overnight before
using to prevent rub-off, and store paper
flat to avoid cracking.

LEFT: Brown paper sponged with copper paint is embellished with copper-dipped galax and lemon leaves, and a metallic ribbon bow. Inexpensive ingredients, yet the result is luxurious.

GILDED LEAVES

Whenever possible, we decorate the house, the tree, and our packages with objects from nature. We have found that leaves dipped in metallic paint make particularly beautiful trimmings, and can also be used to make wrapping paper itself.

For the wrapping paper at left, collect partially dried maple leaves and ferns. Paint one side of leaves with oil-based paint; allow to dry thoroughly. Coat the other side with spray adhesive, and press leaf firmly to colored tissue paper. Wrap gift and tie with organdy ribbon, slipping ribbon through a cluster of Christmas tree balls before as you make the bow.

To make leaf trim, we used bay, galax, and lemon leaves. Holding leaf with chopsticks, dip into paint. Set aside to dry on cake rack. Attach leaves to gift using a hot-glue gun. The store-bought green-and-gold checkered paper at left was adorned with bay leaves in alternating pairs of copper and gold. We have also gilded twigs, pepperberries, and tiny pinecones to use as package trims; simply make sure that any plant material is clean and dry before gilding.

Thin, flexible leaves like maples are best for making the wrapping paper at top. Stiffer leaves make the best trim: we used both fresh and dried bay leaves (far left); galax leaves (being dipped, left); and lemon leaves (drying on kraft paper, right).

RUBBER STAMPS

Custom rubber stamps can be ordered at many stationery stores, and will produce wonderfully individual wrapping paper. The stamps at left were made from photocopies of old engravings and from lettering generated on a desktop computer. Surprisingly, intricate designs translated well to stamps: very simple shapes, in fact, looked slightly crude when transferred to paper. We used metallic ink pads and white or metallic tissue paper. We also made gift tags and cards with the same stamps and soft, handmade paper.

Consider the texture of a gift wrap as well as the appearance. The shimmering, slightly metallic tissue paper wrapping the boxes at left is soft to the touch, as is the complementary wide gilt ribbon.

Moiré ribbon has a shimmering watermark finish and enough body for perfect bows.

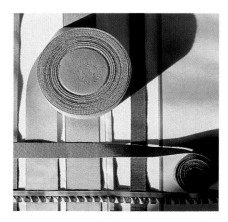

Grosgrain and faille have crosswise ribs, fatter in grosgrain, and subtle elasticity.

Organdy can be floppy or crisp, and is sometimes trimmed with passementerie.

Velvet's plush pile gives ribbons real heft, suitable for hatbands as well as bows.

Black and white ribbons have graphic punch. The lariat design is woven cotton.

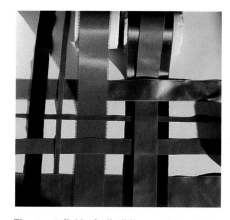

The most fluid of all ribbons, satin is easy to handle and adds a nice note of luxury.

Picot, or feather edging, delicately looped threadwork, appears on all types of ribbon.

Taffeta ribbon, made of very finely woven silk or rayon, is both crisp and delicate.

"Novelty" ribbons like these can lend a wonderfully individual touch to a package.

Classic Cookies

PHOTOGRAPHS BY ANTOINE BOOTZ

WE'VE BEEN PRACTICING OUR COOKIE BAKING SINCE *childhood, so we have amassed quite a collection of tried and true recipes. Here are two dozen of our favorites, from chunky oatmeal fruit drops to delicate rolled and cut sugar cookies. And since a lick at the icing bowl is a holiday ritual, we have also included our best cookie decorating ideas.*

Iced Sugar Cookies

MAKES ABOUT 2 DOZEN

This is the best cookie dough for cutting intricate shapes: even rolled very thin, it is sturdy and holds its shape.

8	tablespoons (1 stick) unsalted butter
1	cup sugar
2	cups sifted all-purpose flour
¼	teaspoon salt
½	teaspoon baking powder
1	large egg, lightly beaten
2	tablespoons brandy (optional)
½	teaspoon vanilla extract

1. Cream together butter and sugar until fluffy. Sift together dry ingredients; add to butter mixture and beat well. Add egg, brandy if desired, and vanilla, and beat again until well mixed.
2. Chill dough for at least 1 hour.
3. Heat oven to 350°.
4. Roll dough ⅛ inch thick. Cut into shapes; leftover dough can be rolled and cut once more.
5. Bake for 10 minutes; do not brown. Remove to wire racks to cool.

ROYAL ICING

1	cup sifted confectioners' sugar
1	large egg white
	Food coloring

Mix together confectioners' sugar and egg white; divide among small bowls and tint each a different color. Spread or pipe onto the cooled cookies and allow to set.

Honey Lebkuchen

MAKES ABOUT 12 DOZEN

Made from an old German recipe, lebkuchen can be iced, but they are rich enough to serve undecorated too.

1½	cups sugar
⅔	cup honey
8	tablespoons (1 stick) unsalted butter
6	cups sifted all-purpose flour
½	teaspoon salt
1½	teaspoons baking soda
¼	teaspoon ground ginger

1 teaspoon cinnamon
  Zest of 1 lemon
½ cup blanched almonds, finely chopped
2 small eggs, lightly beaten

1. Dissolve sugar with honey and butter over low heat. Sift together flour, salt, baking soda, and spices. Add to honey mixture and stir until blended. Stir in the zest, almonds, and eggs.
2. Chill dough for several hours.
3. Heat oven to 350°.
4. Roll dough ¼ inch thick and cut into shapes.
5. Bake for 10 to 12 minutes; remove to wire racks to cool.

German Butter Cookies

MAKES ABOUT 12 DOZEN

An old-fashioned cookie that can be rolled and cut and still has a nice, light texture after baking.

1 cup granulated sugar
1 cup sifted confectioners' sugar
½ pound (2 sticks) unsalted butter
1 cup vegetable oil
2 large eggs, lightly beaten
1 teaspoon vanilla extract
5½ cups sifted all-purpose flour
1 teaspoon cream of tartar
1 teaspoon baking soda

1. Cream together sugars and butter. Add oil; blend in eggs and vanilla. Beat well. Sift together flour, cream of tartar, and baking soda. Add to sugar mixture, beat again.
2. Chill dough for at least 6 hours.
3. Heat oven to 350°.
4. Roll dough ¼ inch thick and cut into shapes.
5. Bake for 8 to 10 minutes; remove to wire racks to cool.
NOTE: Cookies can be decorated with Royal Icing (see page 72) and sprinkled with colored sugars.

Rolled cookies can be cut out and decorated to suit any fancy. OPPOSITE, ABOVE: Sugar cookies get a base coat of thin royal icing and squiggles of chocolate; BELOW: German butter cookies have a base coat of royal icing topped with colored sugars.

FOR PERFECT COOKIES

1. Ingredients really make a difference. Use the best unsalted butter, AAA eggs, unbleached all-purpose flour, coarse salt, and fresh spices. Replace leavening agents often (baking powder loses its effectiveness after about one year). Buy whole, fresh nuts and grind or chop them yourself. Find really good chocolate by the bar and chop, rather than buying chips by the bag.

2. Invest in good, basic equipment: a heavy-duty electric mixer (never mix cookies in a food processor), a small coffee grinder for spices, and heavy baking sheets with low or no sides.

3. Read the ingredient list carefully, and assemble everything before you begin. Follow instructions exactly: if the ingredient list specifies a measure of sifted flour, sift before measuring or you will have too much flour and a stiff dough.

4. If dough is to be rolled, shaped, or cut, form into a flat round, wrap in plastic or wax paper, and chill until firm. For rolling, dust a flat surface (a marble slab is best) with sifted flour; brush excess off dough with a soft bristle brush.

5. Instead of coating baking sheets with butter, cover them with parchment paper. When you take the cookies out of the oven, let cool a little then lift the parchment, cookies and all, off the baking sheets and onto cooling racks.

SUGAR COOKIE WREATH

1. Make Iced Sugar Cookie dough (see page 72); chill and roll out as directed.

2. Cut out dough in leaf shapes. (We used a holly-shape cutter that Martha found in a Japanese hardware store. Shapes can also be cut freehand with a sharp knife, or you can cut a stencil from cardboard and cut around it.)

3. Arrange leaves in an eight-inch circle on a parchment-lined baking sheet. Place so that each leaf slightly overlaps the next; if desired, place additional leaves at intervals around the outer edge.

4. Bake at 350° for 10 minutes; do not allow to brown. Let cool on a rack.

5. Make one recipe Royal Icing (page 72). Divide among three small bowls and tint dark, medium, and light green. Apply a thin base coat of light green, add shadows of medium green. Allow icing to harden, then pipe on "veins" of the dark icing.

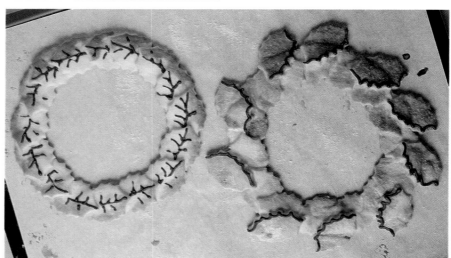

COOKIE CUTTERS

The oldest cookie cutters we know of were made from scraps of tin by itinerant metalsmiths. By the mid-nineteenth century, cutters were mass-produced, and the familiar shapes—animals, stars, flowers, and houses—became popular.

For unusual cutters, search tag sales. If you find a lovely shape but the cutter is worn and scratched, remember it can be retinned. For more individual cutters, make them yourself. Trace a shape onto stiff cardboard and then cut it out. Place the silhouette on rolled-out dough, and incise with a knife around the outline. (Moravian folk artists make cookie cutters in the shape of hands, or the traditional "heart-in-hand" pattern, below. Children can follow their example by tracing their hands onto card, making truly personalized cookie cutters.)

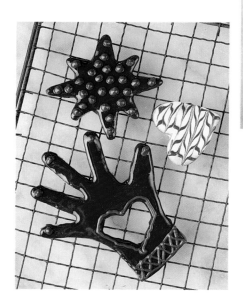

LEFT: Gingerbread cookies were dipped in melted chocolate, or drizzled with chocolate over wet icing (make the zigzags with the point of a knife). ABOVE: Chocolate orange cookies were piped with cooled melted chocolate. OPPOSITE: Butter cream cookies.

Butter Cream Cookies with Chestnut Filling

MAKES ABOUT 30

This rich cookie with its delicious chestnut filling is based on a traditional French recipe.

12	tablespoons (1½ sticks) unsalted butter
¾	cup sifted confectioners' sugar
1	large egg
1½	cups sifted all-purpose flour
½	teaspoon salt

1. Cream butter. Add confectioners' sugar and beat until smooth. Stir in egg. Sift together flour and salt; add to butter mixture and beat well.
2. Chill dough until firm.
3. Heat oven to 350°.
4. Roll dough ⅛ inch thick and then cut into shapes.
5. Bake for 12 minutes; remove to wire racks to cool.

CHESTNUT FILLING

4	tablespoons (½ stick) unsalted butter
⅔	cup sifted confectioners' sugar
	Pinch of salt
2	tablespoons chestnut cream (crème de marrons)

1. Cream butter. Add sugar, salt, and chestnut cream and beat until smooth.
2. Spread filling between two baked and cooled butter-cream cookies.

CHOCOLATE GLAZE

6	ounces semisweet chocolate

Melt chocolate slowly over low heat. Dip filled cookies into warm melted chocolate and allow to set.

Chocolate Orange Cookies

MAKES ABOUT 3 DOZEN

Chocolate and orange is one of those magical combinations that enhances the flavor of both elements without disguising either.

8	tablespoons (1 stick) unsalted butter
⅔	cup sugar
1	large egg
	Zest of 1 orange
1	tablespoon orange-flavored liqueur
1¾	cups sifted all-purpose flour
1	teaspoon baking powder
	Pinch of salt
½	cup grated semisweet chocolate

1. Cream together butter and sugar. Beat in egg, zest, and liqueur. Mix until smooth. Sift together flour, baking powder, and salt, and add slowly to butter mixture. Beat in chocolate.
2. Chill dough for several hours.
3. Heat oven to 325°.
4. Roll dough ¼ inch thick and cut into shapes.
5. Bake for 15 minutes, or until golden. Remove to wire racks to cool.

For chocolate frosting, place good-quality chocolate in a dry metal bowl over hot (not boiling) water, just until melted. Dip cookie in melted chocolate, or allow chocolate to cool until slightly thickened, then pipe through a small round tip.

DECORATING COOKIES

Many of our Christmas cookies were decorated with old-fashioned royal icing, which hardens as it dries: a thin coating on a cookie makes a good foundation for further decorating, and piped royal icing retains its shape perfectly.

To use Royal Icing (see page 72), first mix it to the right consistency, thin for coating, thicker for piping. To tint it, we use paste coloring. Available in most baking-supply stores, it comes in a wider spectrum of colors than liquid coloring. More concentrated than liquid, it should be added to icing one dab at a time with the end of a toothpick and mixed in well.

To give a cookie an even coat, put a spoonful of thin icing at the center. Spread using an icing spatula, the back of a spoon, or (if the shape is intricate and the icing very thin) a pastry brush.

To pipe decorations onto cookies, you'll need either a pastry bag (a ready-made cloth or plastic bag fitted with a plastic coupler and a tip) or a metal forcing tube and plunger assembly. (Professional bakers like Patti Paige, right, prefer the bag; for the less proficient, the metal assembly offers more control.) Whichever method you use, you'll achieve the best results if you rest the tip on your index finger, and push the icing out gently with your thumb.

Patti Paige's Gingerbread

25 GINGERBREAD MEN

New York baker Patti Paige has developed a sturdy gingerbread dough that can be rolled and cut by small children— and still produces a delicious cookie.

10½ tablespoons (1 stick plus 2½ tablespoons) unsalted butter
½ cup firmly packed light brown sugar
2 teaspoons ground ginger
1 teaspoon cinnamon
¼ teaspoon ground cloves
1½ teaspoons salt
1 large egg
¾ cup dark molasses
3 cups sifted all-purpose flour
1 teaspoon baking soda
½ teaspoon baking powder

1. Cream together butter and sugar. Add spices, salt, egg, and molasses, and beat well. Sift together flour, baking soda, and baking powder; add to butter mixture and beat again.
2. Chill dough for several hours.
3. Heat oven to 350°.
4. Roll dough ¼ inch thick. Cut into shapes.
5. Bake for 8 to 10 minutes; remove to wire racks to cool.

Bourbon Currant Cookies

MAKES ABOUT 6 DOZEN

These dense, rich cookies need no frosting or decoration, just a brush of egg glaze before baking.

½ pound (2 sticks) unsalted butter
1 cup sugar
1 large egg
3 cups sifted all-purpose flour
⅓ cup bourbon
½ cup dried currants
1 large egg lightly beaten with 4 tablespoons heavy cream, for glaze

1. Heat oven to 350°.
2. Cream together butter and sugar. Add egg, flour, bourbon, and currants; mix well.
3. Roll dough ¼ inch thick and cut into desired shapes. Brush cookies with egg-glaze mixture.
4. Bake for 12 to 15 minutes; remove to wire racks to cool.

Chocolate Charms

MAKES ABOUT 5 DOZEN

For those who love truffles, here is the perfect cookie: rich in flavor, but light in texture.

3 ounces semisweet chocolate
1 tablespoon orange-flavored liqueur
½ pound (2 sticks) unsalted butter
1 cup sugar
3 large eggs
3½ cups sifted all-purpose flour
2 teaspoons baking powder
¼ teaspoon baking soda
Sifted Dutch-processed cocoa powder, for rolling

1. Heat oven to 350°.
2. Melt chocolate over low heat. Cool slightly and stir in liqueur. Cream together butter and sugar. Add eggs one at a time, blending well. Sift together dry ingredients and add to butter mixture. Stir in melted chocolate and blend well.
3. Form dough into 1-inch balls and roll in cocoa powder.
4. Bake for 8 to 10 minutes. Remove to wire racks to cool, and roll again in cocoa powder.

Peanut Butter Cookies

MAKES ABOUT 4 DOZEN

This is a very good cookie to make with children: they enjoy forming the little pats of dough in their hands, and pressing them with a fork for decoration—and they love the peanut-butter taste.

8	tablespoons (1 stick) unsalted butter
1	cup firmly packed light brown sugar
1	large egg
½	teaspoon vanilla extract
1	cup smooth peanut butter
1½	cups sifted all-purpose flour
¼	teaspoon salt
1	teaspoon baking soda

1. Cream together butter and sugar. Add egg and vanilla and beat. Add peanut butter and beat again. Sift together dry ingredients and add to butter mixture; beat again until smooth.
2. Chill dough for several hours.
3. Heat oven to 350°.
4. Form dough into 1½-inch balls and press down slightly with palm of hand. Use the tines of a fork to decorate edges.
5. Bake for 10 minutes; remove to wire racks to cool.

Some cookies are so rich in flavor and texture they need little or no decoration. Chocolate charms, opposite, have just a dusting of cocoa powder. Bourbon currant cookies, above, are glazed before baking; peanut butter cookies, left, can be edged with a little melted chocolate.

Oatmeal Fruit Cookies

MAKES ABOUT 4 DOZEN

This is the best-ever version of the traditional oatmeal-raisin cookie: chewy, spicy, and filled with fruit.

4	tablespoons (½ stick) unsalted butter
1	cup firmly packed dark brown sugar
½	cup granulated sugar
1	large egg
⅔	cup milk
1	teaspoon vanilla extract
1½	cups sifted all-purpose flour
1	teaspoon baking soda
1	teaspoon cinnamon
¼	teaspoon ground cloves
¼	teaspoon ground nutmeg
3	cups rolled oats
1	cup dried fruit such as figs, apples, and apricots
1	cup raisins

1. Cream together butter, sugars, egg, milk, and vanilla. Sift together flour, baking soda, and spices, and add to butter mixture. Stir in oats, mixing well. Stir in dried fruit and raisins.
2. Chill dough for several hours.
3. Heat oven to 350°.
4. Drop batter by teaspoonfuls, about 2 inches apart, onto baking sheets.
5. Bake for 12 minutes; remove to wire racks to cool.

DROP COOKIES

Rolled, cut, and decorated cookies are the prettiest. But old-fashioned drop cookies, like our oatmeal fruit cookies, above, are sometimes more satisfying, and always faster to produce. Make double batches of dough, and freeze, well wrapped, for up to a month. Thaw before use, then drop by the spoonful, well spaced, onto parchment-lined baking sheet.

Ginger Crinkles

MAKES ABOUT 4 DOZEN

Like English ginger biscuits, our crinkles have a spicy flavor and crunchy texture.

12	tablespoons (1½ sticks) unsalted butter
1	cup sugar
¼	cup dark molasses
1	large egg, lightly beaten
2	cups sifted all-purpose flour
3	teaspoons baking soda
¼	teaspoon salt
1	teaspoon ground cloves
1½	teaspoons cinnamon
1½	teaspoons ground ginger
	Extra sugar, for rolling

1. Cream together butter and sugar until fluffy. Blend in molasses and egg. Sift together dry ingredients; add to butter mixture and beat well.
2. Chill dough for at least 1 hour.
3. Heat oven to 350°.
4. Form dough into 1-inch balls and roll in sugar.
5. Bake for 8 to 10 minutes. Let cool on baking sheets for at least 3 minutes, until cookies are set.

Ne Plus Ultra Cookies

MAKES ABOUT 1 DOZEN

Our Webster's Dictionary *defines "ne plus ultra" as "the peak of achievement." These cookies begin as traditional chocolate chip, and are enhanced with raisins and pecans.*

8	tablespoons (1 stick) unsalted butter
⅔	cup firmly packed dark brown sugar
¼	cup granulated sugar
1	teaspoon vanilla extract
2	large eggs
1¼	cups sifted all-purpose flour
½	teaspoon salt
½	teaspoon baking soda
1	cup semisweet chocolate chips
1	cup raisins
1	cup pecans, coarsely chopped

1. Heat oven to 350°.
2. Cream together butter and sugars until fluffy. Add vanilla and eggs; beat well. Sift together flour, salt, and baking soda; add to butter mixture. Beat again. Stir in chocolate chips, raisins, and pecans.
3. Form dough into 2½-inch balls, and press to 1 inch thick with palm of hand.
4. Bake for 20 minutes, or until golden. Remove to wire racks to cool.

Cassis Crisps

MAKES ABOUT 2½ DOZEN

The cassis (black-currant-flavored liqueur) or black-currant juice lends these cookies a beautiful, faintly lavender tint.

8	tablespoons (1 stick) unsalted butter
1	cup sugar
2	large eggs
2	tablespoons cassis or black-currant juice
2¾	cups sifted all-purpose flour
2	teaspoons baking powder
½	teaspoon salt
	Colored sugar, for decorating

1. Cream together butter and sugar until fluffy. Add eggs and cassis or juice. Sift together dry ingredients and add to butter mixture, beating until smooth.
2. Chill dough for several hours.
3. Heat oven to 350°.
4. Roll dough ¼ inch thick and cut into shapes. Sprinkle with colored sugar.
5. Bake for 8 to 10 minutes; remove to wire racks to cool.

OPPOSITE, ABOVE: Chunky oatmeal fruit cookies; BELOW: Ginger crinkles. LEFT: Cassis crisps. ABOVE: The cookie that Martha dubbed the "ne plus ultra." They are so good we like to make them extra large.

We cut our shortbread into bars,
which were then scored and decorated with the tines of a fork.
Shortbread can also be cut into
shapes, or pressed into molds
(make sure it's no more than a
quarter inch thick, though), or
baked in a big round.

Coconut Almond Cookies

MAKES ABOUT 3 DOZEN

A cookie with complex, nutty flavors, topped with almond icing and a tangle of coconut.

1	cup finely shredded coconut
½	pound (2 sticks) unsalted butter
¼	teaspoon salt
½	cup sifted confectioners' sugar
1	teaspoon almond extract
2¼	cups sifted cake flour
¾	cup blanched almonds, finely ground

1. Toast shredded coconut by spreading in a thin layer on cookie sheet and baking in a 325° oven until light golden brown, about 20 minutes. Stir occasionally.
2. Cream butter with salt. Gradually add sugar, beating until fluffy. Add almond extract and toasted coconut. Add flour, a little at a time. Stir in almonds.
3. Chill dough for several hours.
4. Heat oven to 325°.
5. Roll dough ¼ inch thick and cut into shapes.
6. Bake for 18 to 20 minutes; remove to wire racks to cool.

ALMOND BUTTER CREAM ICING

½	cup (1 stick) unsalted butter
1	cup sifted confectioners' sugar
¼	teaspoon salt
1	teaspoon almond extract
1	cup toasted coconut

Cream butter. Add sugar and salt. Beat until fluffy. Stir in almond extract. Spread on cookies and top with coconut.

Espresso Shortbread

MAKES ABOUT 2 DOZEN

A simple shortbread with a sophisticated coffee flavor.

½	pound (2 sticks) unsalted butter
½	cup firmly packed light brown sugar
1	teaspoon vanilla extract
¾	teaspoon powdered instant coffee
2¼	cups sifted all-purpose flour
¼	teaspoon salt

1. Cream together butter and sugar until fluffy. Add vanilla and coffee. Sift together flour and salt; add to butter mixture and beat well.
2. Chill dough until firm.
3. Heat oven to 325°.
4. Roll dough ¼ inch thick and cut into 2-inch-by-5-inch bars. Prick with a fork. Score middles of bars with a knife.
5. Bake for 20 to 25 minutes, or until light golden brown. Remove to wire racks to cool.

We topped coconut almond cookies with coconut shredded at home. Drain a fresh coconut by piercing one of the "eyes" with a screwdriver. Tap bottom end (away from eyes) until a piece breaks off. Continue tapping around broken edge of shell until it begins to break apart (it should spiral off following a natural fault line). Pry the white meat from the shell, remove the brown skin from the meat with a vegetable peeler, then grate the meat.

Polish Tea Cookies

MAKES ABOUT 2 DOZEN

From a Kostyra family recipe. At Christmastime, we make and store a big tin full of these cookies, filling them with homemade jams just before serving.

8	tablespoons (1 stick) unsalted butter
¾	cup sugar
1	large egg yolk, lightly beaten
1	teaspoon vanilla extract
1	cup sifted all-purpose flour
1	cup blanched almonds, finely ground
	Extra sugar, for rolling
1	large egg white, lightly beaten
	Jam, for filling

1. Cream together butter and sugar. Add egg yolk and vanilla; beat well. Add flour; beat again.
2. Chill dough for several hours.
3. Heat oven to 325°.
4. Combine almonds with two tablespoons sugar. Form dough into small balls and dip in beaten egg white, then in almond-sugar mixture. Press center of each ball with your thumb.
5. Bake for 5 minutes, then remove and push down centers again. Bake for another 15 minutes, or until golden brown. Cool slightly on wire racks and fill centers with jam.

Mocha Almond Cookies

MAKES ABOUT 2 DOZEN

Dark chocolate dough is rolled in sugar; as it bakes, the sugar will "crackle," exposing the bittersweet cookie within.

4	ounces unsweetened chocolate
8	tablespoons (1 stick) unsalted butter
6	tablespoons coffee-flavored liqueur
2	large eggs
¾	cup sugar
1⅓	cups sifted all-purpose flour
¾	teaspoon baking powder
1	cup blanched almonds, finely ground
	Extra sugar, for rolling
	Sifted confectioners' sugar, for rolling

1. Melt together chocolate and butter over low heat, stir in coffee liqueur; keep mixture warm. Beat together eggs and sugar until fluffy. Stir flavored chocolate into the egg mixture. Sift together flour and baking powder; stir into chocolate-and-egg mixture and beat well. Stir in ground almonds.
2. Chill dough until firm. Form dough into 1-inch balls and chill again for 10 minutes.
3. Heat oven to 325°.
4. Roll balls first in granulated sugar and then in confectioners' sugar, coating well.
5. Bake for 15 minutes; remove to wire racks to cool.

Lemon Cream Cheese Bows

MAKES ABOUT 5 DOZEN

We baked these cookies in a bow shape, but they could also be piped into wreaths, numbers, or letters of the alphabet.

½	pound (2 sticks) unsalted butter
1	3-ounce package cream cheese
1	cup sugar
1	large egg
1	teaspoon finely chopped lemon zest
2	tablespoons fresh lemon juice
3	cups sifted all-purpose flour
1	teaspoon baking powder
	Confectioner' sugar, for sprinkling.

1. Cream together butter and cream cheese. Beat in sugar. Add egg, lemon zest, and lemon juice; mix well. Sift together flour and baking powder; work into butter mixture.
2. Chill dough for several hours.
3. Heat oven to 375°.
4. Using a pastry bag with a star tip, pipe dough into bows.
5. Bake for 8 to 10 minutes. Cool on racks and sprinkle with confectioners' sugar.

Pistachio Lemon Drops

MAKES ABOUT 2 DOZEN

A cross between a macaroon and a cookie.

1	large egg white
	Pinch of salt
1	cup unsalted pistachio nuts, finely chopped
1	cup firmly packed light brown sugar
1	tablespoon all-purpose flour
½	teaspoon fresh lemon juice

1. Heat oven to 325°.
2. Beat egg white with salt until stiff. Add nuts and sugar and mix well. Add flour and lemon juice; beat to blend well.
3. Drop batter by teaspoonfuls onto baking sheets.
4. Bake for 10 minutes, until light brown. Cool on racks.

OPPOSITE, ABOVE: Jam-filled Polish tea cookies; **BELOW:** Mocha almond cookies. **ABOVE RIGHT:** Lemon cream cheese bows, with a heavy dusting of confectioners' sugar. **RIGHT:** Pistachio lemon drops, to which we added a thin curl of lemon peel.

Black Pepper Cookies

MAKES ABOUT 5 DOZEN

This cookie's odd ingredients lend it an indefinable spiciness.

½ pound (2 sticks) unsalted butter
1 cup sugar
1 cup dark corn syrup
1 tablespoon cider vinegar
5 cups sifted all-purpose flour
1 teaspoon baking soda
1¼ teaspoons cinnamon
1¼ teaspoons ground ginger
1 teaspoon ground cloves
½ teaspoon freshly ground pepper
2 large eggs, lightly beaten
   Colored sugar, for decoration

1. Melt butter, sugar, syrup, and vinegar over low heat and let cool. Sift together dry ingredients; stir into butter mixture. Beat in eggs, mixing until batter is very smooth.
2. Chill dough for several hours.
3. Heat oven to 350°. Divide dough into four equal portions. Working with one portion at a time, roll dough ⅛ inch thick. Cut into shapes and sprinkle with colored sugars.
4. Bake for 7 to 8 minutes; remove to wire racks to cool.

Buttery Pecan Rounds

MAKES ABOUT 3 DOZEN

This is a wonderfully simple drop cookie with a real nutty flavor.

½ pound (2 sticks) unsalted butter
¾ cup firmly packed dark brown sugar
1 large egg yolk
1 cup sifted all-purpose flour
½ teaspoon salt
⅔ cup chopped pecans
   Pecan halves, for decorating

1. Heat oven to 325°.
2. Cream together butter and sugar. Add egg yolk. Sift together flour and salt; add to butter mixture and beat well. Stir in chopped pecans.
3. Drop batter by teaspoonfuls onto a baking sheet. Press one pecan half into the center of each cookie.
4. Bake for 12 to 15 minutes; remove to wire racks to cool.

Biscochitos

MAKES ABOUT 4 DOZEN

Aniseed adds an old-world flavor to this crunchy cookies.

½ pound (2 sticks) unsalted butter
¾ cup sugar
1 teaspoon aniseed
1 large egg
2 tablespoons tequila (optional)
2½ cups sifted all-purpose flour
1½ teaspoons baking powder
½ teaspoon salt
¼ teaspoon ground cardamom
2 tablespoons sugar mixed with ½ teaspoon cinnamon

1. Cream together butter and sugar. Add aniseed and mix well. Beat in egg and tequila if desired. Sift together dry ingredients except cinnamon-sugar mixture and stir into batter; beat well.
2. Chill dough until firm.
3. Heat oven to 350°. Roll dough ¼ inch thick and cut into shapes. Sprinkle with cinnamon sugar.
4. Bake for about 12 minutes; remove to wire racks to cool.

Mazurka with Apricot Topping

MAKES 3 DOZEN WEDGES

Another Kostyra family recipe, this cookie is named for the Mazurka—a Polish dance rather like the polka.

½ pound (2 sticks) unsalted butter
1½ cups sifted all-purpose flour
1 cup sugar
½ teaspoon salt
6 large egg yolks
½ cup blanched almonds, finely ground
  Zest of 1 orange or lemon

1. Heat oven to 325°. Butter two 10-inch round cake pans and line with parchment paper. Set aside.
2. Cream butter until fluffy. Sift together flour, sugar, and salt and add to butter, alternating with the egg yolks. Beat until well mixed. Carefully stir in almonds and citrus zest.
3. Pat dough into prepared pans.
4. Bake for 35 to 40 minutes, until golden brown; remove to wire racks to cool.

APRICOT TOPPING

1 cup apricot jam
2 tablespoons orange-flavored liqueur

Heat jam gently. Add liqueur. Strain warm glaze through a fine sieve and spread atop cooled mazurka rounds.

OPPOSITE, ABOVE: Crisp black-pepper fish; BELOW: Buttery pecan rounds. ABOVE RIGHT: Wedges of mazurka topped with apricot. ABOVE: Animal-shaped biscochitos.

Wreaths and Garlands

EVERGREENS ARE INDEED BEAUTIFUL, BUT THE *American landscape is so full, even in the bleakest Northern winter, of other scents, colors, shapes, and textures it seems a shame to limit wreaths to just the pines and hollies. In parts of this country, the growing season extends right to Christmas: California's hills, for example, are still green.*

Look in your garden, gather what you can, and you may find yourself making wreaths of bay, quince, olive, or even cactus, garlands of magnolia, arches of hawthorn and viburnum. Bring it indoors: a wreath can hang on a curtain as well as a door—it can even serve as a tieback. It can frame a mirror, arch over a doorway, or serve as centerpiece.

Fruited branches frame an old mirror. OPPOSITE: A wreath of oak leaves and acorns is light enough to hang on a curtain.

OAK-AND-ACORN WREATH: For a twelve-inch wreath form, you'll need at least twenty pressed oak leaves and several branches covered with acorns. Twist short wires around leaf bases to extend stems. Wrap stems around metal wreath form at regular intervals. With a hot-glue gun, dot wrapped joints with glue; press on acorn branches and hold in place until glue is dry.

FRUITED FRAME

The fruited frame shown on the previous page is built using a basic wreath-making technique: wiring bunches of foliage to a metal form which can be purchased from a crafts store.

You'll need a rectangular double flat wreath form (two forms an inch apart in size that have been welded together); branches of olive, bay, pittosporum, and fig bearing green fruit; unripe quinces and persimmons, wire cutters; gardening clippers; and twenty-two-gauge floral wire, wound on a paddle. At a corner of the wreath form, anchor one end of the wire with a few twists. Create a small bunch of olive, bay, and pittosporum about ten inches high; fan it out evenly and flatten on one side. Position the bunch on wreath form at wired corner and wire in place with five tight wraps. It must be tightly wired, because deciduous foliage will shrink as it dries and will loosen. Wire on a second mixed bunch so that its branches cover wire stems. Continue until form is finished. To attach fruit, pierce each near the stem with U-shaped floral pins, and bind around frame so that fruit nestles among greenery. (Figs should be wired by the branch, not by piercing.) Hung in a cool place, the frame should look fresh for about three weeks.

MAGNOLIA TIEBACK

1. Double a piece of heavy floral wire to desired length to make tieback base. At doubled end, knot the wire an inch in. Poke floral wire mounted on a paddle through hole in knot and twist it back on itself to anchor.

2. Bunch together a few branches of magnolia and privet, the privet stripped of all but opened fruit. Using paddle, wire branches tightly to tieback base at knot. Continue wiring on greenery, positioning bunches to alternate sides as you go. Stop three inches short of the end; twist the base wire ends together and form a loop for hanging.

3. From the back, bind to secure the greenery.

Wreath forms come in a variety of shapes, sizes, and materials. We used four different kinds here: vine, metal, foam, and straw, each chosen to suit its purpose and decorations.

GRAPEVINE WREATH

The wreath of twisted, dried grape vines, above far left, is a country classic, and a base for endless variation. Thomas Pritchard and William Jarecki at Pure Mädderlake, the New York florist, weave in mimosa and heather, but one could add any dried flower, evergreen, or berry. Those with strong stems can be simply poked into the form and secured between two twigs of vine. More delicate blooms can be attached with thin wire.

OAK LEAF WREATH

For the wreath shown near left, above, we used about three hundred oak leaves still on the branch, gathered after they'd turned gold. By using leaves on the branch, you can get a much fuller wreath, with realistic variations in leaf size. Following the basic wreath-building technique described on page 92 for the fruited frame, create small bunches of leafy branches, flatten on one side, and wire one after another to an eighteen-inch double flat wreath form until entire form is thickly covered. (If you are lucky enough to gather oak sprigs with acorns still attached, make sure they remain visible among the leaves.)

FLOWER WREATHS

The circle of dried flowers at bottom far left was created at New York's Beautiful Flowers. A circle of Oasis foam was thickly studded with dried hydrangeas, chenille plants, and peonies; any other dried flowers could be substituted. Twigs, another New York florist, makes a version of this wreath using fresh roses and sweet peas. The Oasis is soaked in water for several hours. The rose stems are clipped to three or four inches and pushed into the foam until every scrap of foam is covered. Not an ornament to be hung, this wreath, in a waterproof tray or on a platter, makes a charming, scented centerpiece. Keep in a cool spot (in the refrigerator at night, if possible) and mist frequently over the two or three days the wreath will last.

PRICKLY PEAR WREATH

Paperwhite in New York made the wreath with the Western spirit, below near left, out of cactus pads, or *nopales,* which can be purchased at many Hispanic grocery stores. Wearing heavy garden gloves and handling the cactus pads with tongs whenever possible (those spines are extremely sharp), fix each pad to the form with a hot-glue gun. For extra security, attach the stem-end of the pad to the form with a U-shape floral pin. Repeat process with the next pad, and continue until the form is covered.

Once each wreath form has been completely covered by its decorations, turn it over and trim off protruding stems with secateurs so that the wreath will lie flat against wall or door. Attach a loop of wire, threading it well into the form, and hang from the smallest nail that will secure it.

A GLOSSARY OF GREENERY

The idea of using what we can find, rather than what we already know, can be a liberating one in holiday decorating. A walk in the woods, even a trip to the back yard, can turn up leaves, branches, fruit, and nuts that work well ornamentally. (An outing to the park or the roadside may also yield results, but one is limited to greenery that has already fallen.)

Although many of the plants we used here may not be seasonal throughout the country, cuttings are available by mail order from northern California, where the growing season is extended, and where heavy pruning of even wild shrubs is encouraged to reduce the risk of fire.

Berried branches will hold up well for about three weeks; leathery leaves such as magnolia and ivy will last about the same. The more humid your home, the longer any cut greenery will last. (Misting daily with water helps.) Both berries and leaves will shrink slightly as they dry out but will hold their color beautifully.

On the opposite page, a glossary of our new materials: 1. Pittosporum 2. Bay 3. Hydrangea 4. Olive 5. Ivy 6. Wild rose hip 7. Privet 8. Persimmon 9. Pyracantha 10. Magnolia 11. Flowering plum 12. Oak 13. Rain tree 14. Hawthorn 15. Lady crab apple 16. Grape 17. Quince 18. Pistachio 19. Viburnum 20. Lady apple 21. Fig 22. Snowdrift crab apple.

FRUITED WREATH: Although it's built on a double flat wreath form just six inches across, this wreath is so full that its finished diameter is fourteen inches. Make it by following the instructions for the fruited frame, using any mix of small fruits; we combined fig branches, pittosporum, pistachio, and pyracantha, all trimmed of their leaves.

Cornmeal pancakes have the nutty flavor of whole grain without its heaviness. OPPOSITE: Mixed citrus salad in a footed compote dish is an elegant alternative to simple grapefruit halves.

Family Breakfast

PHOTOGRAPHS BY TODD EBERLE

BRITISH WRITER JANE GRIGSON ONCE CAUTIONED *the holiday cook, "Don't try to be original. In my experience, clever food is not appreciated at Christmas. It makes the little ones cry and the old ones nervous." That may be so at dinnertime, when cultural expectations call for the roast bird and the flaming pudding, but at breakfast we're free to make our own traditions. For every family that starts the day around a table set with Christmas china and laden with bacon and eggs, there's another that feasts on foil-wrapped chocolate Santas straight from the stocking. Our preference is for the middle ground: a breakfast that's hearty but not heavy, quick to make and just enough to sustain us through the day's activities until it's time for dinner. And that leaves us with just one great question: Shall we open the gifts before or after breakfast? Again, every family makes its own tradition. Bowing to the wishes of the children, we open our presents beforehand, of course.*

FRESH FRUIT JUICE

Some of our recipes demand "freshly squeezed juice." There is no substitute. No matter how hard they try, manufacturers cannot get the taste of fresh fruit into bottles, cans, cartons, or those little plastic lemons and limes. We use an old-fashioned Hamilton Beach juicer to squeeze our fruit; we find there is less waste than with more complicated machines. (It even works on pomegranates, producing extraordinary translucent ruby liquid.)

Breakfast Frittata

SERVES 10

This versatile Italian omelet can be made with many different fillings. Leftover frittata should be served at room temperature (with a green salad and good bread, it makes a wonderful lunch).

1	red pepper
12	large eggs, beaten
1	cup milk
¾	cup sliced scallions (about 1 small bunch)
1	tablespoon fresh tarragon, coarsely chopped, plus a few sprigs for garnish
1	teaspoon salt
½	teaspoon freshly ground pepper
5	ounces goat cheese, crumbled
½	tablespoon unsalted butter
½	tablespoon olive oil
2	small red potatoes, sliced ⅛ inch thick

1. Roast, peel, and seed pepper according to directions on page 16. Cut into ¼-inch-wide strips.
2. Combine pepper strips, eggs, milk, most of the scallions, tarragon, salt, pepper, and half of the goat cheese. Set aside.
3. Heat butter and oil in a 10-inch ovenproof sauté pan (preferably nonstick) over medium heat. Add potatoes and cook on both sides until tender, about 8 minutes.
4. Heat oven to 350°. Pour egg mixture over potatoes and cook over medium-low heat, pulling back edges with a rubber spatula until whole frittata is partially cooked, about 8 minutes. Sprinkle remaining cheese over frittata and place in oven. Bake until completely set in center, about 25 minutes. Garnish with tarragon sprigs and remaining scallions. Serve hot, warm, or at room temperature.

Mixed Citrus Salad

SERVES 4

Section four whole pink or white grapefruit and four whole oranges. Remove pith and membrane from sections. Place fruit in a large bowl and sprinkle with seeds of half a pomegranate and with 2 or 3 crushed brown sugar cubes. Serve chilled.

Cornmeal Pancakes
with Cranberry Maple Compote

MAKES NINE 5-INCH PANCAKES

For "instant" homemade pancakes, mix dry ingredients and store in an airtight container. Combine with liquid just before cooking.

- ¾ cup all-purpose flour
- 2 tablespoons sugar
- ½ cup yellow cornmeal
- 4 teaspoons baking powder
- ¾ teaspoon salt
- 1 cup milk
- 5 tablespoons unsalted butter
- 2 large eggs, beaten
-   Vegetable oil

1. In a large bowl, thoroughly combine flour, sugar, cornmeal, baking powder, and salt.
2. Combine milk and butter in a small saucepan and warm over low heat until butter melts. Let cool to lukewarm, then beat in eggs.
3. Pour wet mixture over dry ingredients and, using a wooden spoon, combine with a few swift strokes. Don't worry if a few lumps remain; they'll work themselves out when cooking.
4. Heat a griddle or skillet over medium heat until hot enough to make a few drops of water bounce. Lightly oil griddle using a brush or paper towel.
5. Spoon enough batter onto griddle to make 5-inch rounds. Cook until bubbles on the surface break and edges begin to look dry, about 2 minutes. Flip pancakes and cook until bottoms brown, about 1 more minute. Continue until all pancakes are made. (You may need to re-oil the griddle between batches of pancakes.) Keep pancakes warm, covered with a kitchen towel, in an oven set at lowest temperature. Serve with butter and warm Cranberry-Maple Compote (recipe follows).

CRANBERRY MAPLE COMPOTE

In a small saucepan, combine 1 cup of fresh cranberries and 1 cup of pure maple syrup. Heat slowly over medium-low heat until mixture comes to a simmer. Cook until cranberries soften and burst and syrup turns red, about 10 minutes. The compote will keep in the refrigerator for up to a week.

ABOVE RIGHT: Frittata combines vegetables with goat cheese and eggs. RIGHT: The citrus salad. Our table was set for breakfast with an Irish linen cloth and old damask napkins.

Christmas Dinner

WE HAVE NEVER QUITE UNDERSTOOD THE CUSTOM OF *serving holiday meals in midafternoon. We know it is based on necessity: before electricity, rural gatherings had to end at dusk so all could return home in safety. But why should that rule still obtain in the holiday season and at no other time? In deference to family wishes, we have now achieved a compromise: Thanksgiving Dinner is served at four o'clock, Christmas Dinner at seven or eight, with guests in formal or at least "proper" dress. We serve a hearty breakfast, a light luncheon, and have time to visit friends for the distribution of gifts, and to take a long, healthful walk in the afternoon, building up our appetites for the meal to come. When we return home, we fill the house with candles against the night, and we celebrate.*

MENU

Roasted Root Vegetables

Loin of Venison with Red-Currant Bordelaise

Citrus Terrine Salad

Rosemary Shallot Popovers

Roast Capon with Wild Rice Sourdough Stuffing

Wild Mushroom and Leek Beggars' Purse

Caramel Coated Seckel Pears

Candied Ginger

Gingerbread

Cranberry Linzer Tarts

Apple Charlotte

PHOTOGRAPHS BY VICTORIA PEARSON

Roasted Root Vegetables

SERVES 8 TO 10

Use any vegetables you wish; our choice is merely an example.

2-3   pounds winter vegetables (we used carrots, turnips,
  rutabagas, parsnips, pearl onions, and potatoes
4   tablespoons (½ stick) unsalted butter, or to taste
¼   cup chicken or veal stock, plus more as needed
  Salt and freshly ground pepper
  Handful of chopped fresh herbs

1. Heat oven to 375°. Scrub vegetables and peel as desired.
Cut into 1- to 2-inch pieces (they should all be of similar size).
2. Melt butter in a roasting pan. Add vegetables, ¼ cup of
stock, and salt and pepper. Stir well and return to oven.
3. Cook vegetables for 1 to 1½ hours, or until vegetables are
tender and golden brown, stirring occasionally and adding
stock as needed to keep vegetables slightly moist. Stir in herbs
and serve immediately.

Loin of Venison with Red Currant Bordelaise

SERVES 8 TO 10

*Many butchers will order venison for you; for a mail-order
source, see "The Guide." Ask for a boneless saddle of venison,
which will yield two loins about two pounds each.*

1   tablespoon juniper berries
1   tablespoon peppercorns
1   tablespoon whole allspice
1   boneless saddle of venison
4   shallots, minced
1   bottle dry red wine
2   cups veal or game stock (see Note)
3   tablespoons red-currant jelly
  Salt and freshly ground pepper
2   teaspoons vegetable oil

1. Combine juniper berries, peppercorns, and allspice in a
spice or coffee grinder and process to a powder. Rub mixture
into meat and refrigerate several hours.
2. Combine shallots and red wine in a medium saucepan.
Bring to a boil; simmer until reduced by three quarters, about
45 minutes. Add stock and bring to a boil again. Simmer until
reduced by half, about 30 minutes. Sauce should be thick
enough to coat the back of a spoon. Stir in jelly and add salt
and pepper to taste; set sauce aside.
3. Heat oven to 400°. Heat oil in a large, heavy skillet over
medium heat. Add venison loins and brown quickly on all
sides. Transfer to a roasting pan; place in oven for 6 to 8 minutes per pound for rare to medium rare.
4. Remove venison from pan and sprinkle lightly with salt.
Let sit for 10 minutes. Slice on an angle and serve with sauce.
NOTE: Many butchers and specialty-food stores sell good-
quality stocks.

**Left: Our main course. Loin of venison with red-currant bordelaise
sauce is accompanied by roasted root vegetables and wild-mushroom-and-leek beggars' purses tied with leek leaf "ribbons."**

Wedgwood manufactured china in the Fallow Deer pattern for only a brief time. It was glazed in both copper and blue luster, and pieces can still be found at the occasional tag or garage sale.

SETTING THE TABLE

Many of us set up house with a full set of china, silver place settings, and an array of appropriate glasses. We laid tables with every item perfectly matched until, little by little, oddities were introduced. A vast old soup tureen found at a tag sale, a set of bone-handled fish knives, amethyst Depression glasses from a consignment shop: our cupboards are crammed with finds and we set the table for each event with pieces chosen for a sensibility. For this Christmas dinner, we chose a 1920s ecru linen tablecloth decorated with an organza appliqué of reindeer and ferns, silver plate chargers topped with antique Wedgwood plates, vintage flatware in several different patterns, and a mix of old and new clear and colored glass.

Citrus Terrine Salad

SERVES 8 TO 10

*The beets, terrine, and dressing can be prepared ahead of time
and assembled at the last minute.*

1	bunch (4 to 6) beets, washed and trimmed
1	teaspoon salt
12	oranges
6	grapefruit, pink and white
1	cup fresh orange juice, strained
1	envelope unflavored gelatin
	Mixed salad greens
	Walnut Vinaigrette (recipe follows)
6	radishes, sliced paper thin

1. Place beets in a small saucepan and cover with cold
water. Add salt and bring to a boil over medium-high heat.
Simmer until tender when pierced with the tip of a knife,
about 30 minutes. Drain and cool. Peel and cut into match-
stick-size pieces.

2. Using a sharp stainless-steel knife, slice off stems and tips
of citrus. Cut away peel and pith in long strokes, following
curve of flesh. Slide knife down one side of a segment, cutting
it away from white membrane. Twist blade under section and
lift out. Continue until all sections are removed.

3. Pour ⅓ cup of the orange juice into a small bowl. Sprinkle
gelatin evenly over surface and let soften for 10 to 15 minutes, stirring once or twice. Heat remaining ⅔ cup juice to a
simmer and combine with gelatin mixture. Stir well until
gelatin has dissolved. Refrigerate until cool to the touch,
about 30 minutes.

4. Line two 6-by-3-inch terrine molds with plastic wrap. Drib-
ble a few tablespoons of gelatin mixture in bottom of molds
and arrange a layer of orange sections in them. Cover with
more spoonfuls of gelatin, and top with a layer of grapefruit
sections going in opposite direction. Repeat until you've
reached top of mold. Do not press down fruit. Fold plastic
wrap over molds and refrigerate overnight.

5. When ready to serve, dip terrine molds into a bowl of hot
water for a few seconds and invert them onto a cutting board.
Remove plastic wrap. Using a serrated or very sharp knife,
carefully cut into ¾-inch slices.

6. Arrange greens on each of 8 plates. Dress beets with some
of the vinaigrette. Top the greens with a slice of terrine and
garnish with beets and radish slices. Drizzle salads with
remaining vinaigrette.

WALNUT VINAIGRETTE

1 teaspoon balsamic vinegar
4 teaspoons fresh orange juice
4 tablespoons walnut oil
Salt and freshly ground pepper

Combine vinegar and orange juice in a small bowl. Whisk in oil. Season to taste with salt and pepper.

Rosemary Shallot Popovers

MAKES 6

To make popovers that really pop over, use a popover frame. A muffin tin is a substitute, but won't produce the best results.

2½ tablespoons plus 1 teaspoon unsalted butter
4 shallots, minced
1 tablespoon chopped fresh rosemary
1½ cups milk
1½ cups all-purpose flour
½ teaspoon salt
4 large eggs

1. Heat oven to 450°. Place rack on bottom level. Rub tins with a little oil and set aside.
2. Heat 1 teaspoon butter in a small sauté pan over low heat. Add shallots and cook until soft and transparent, about 5 minutes. Add rosemary and set aside.
3. Melt 1½ tablespoons butter. Combine with milk, flour, and salt. Beat in eggs one at a time. Add shallots and rosemary.
4. Heat empty tins for 5 minutes; remove from oven. Divide remaining tablespoon butter among tins and heat until butter sizzles. Divide batter evenly among cups.
5. Bake for 20 minutes; turn down heat to 350° without opening oven. Bake 20 minutes more. When done, sides should feel crisp and firm. Poke with a sharp knife to release steam; serve immediately.

OPPOSITE, TOP: Citrus terrine salad on old silver dinner plates; BOTTOM: Swirled beeswax candles are held in crystal candlesticks and massed down the center of the table. ABOVE LEFT: "Ritual is an expression of solidarity," writes Margaret Visser in *The Rituals of Dinner*. LEFT: Rosemary shallot popovers, hot from the oven.

Roast Capon With Wild Rice Sourdough Stuffing

SERVES 8

Capon (a neutered male chicken weighing from six to nine pounds) is a nice alternative to turkey for a small gathering.

2½ cups water
    Salt
1½ cups mixed uncooked wild and brown rice
4 ounces pancetta, cubed (see Note)
2 onions, chopped
5-6 carrots, peeled and chopped
4 ribs celery, chopped
    Freshly ground pepper
1½ cups chicken stock, plus up to 1 cup more
¼ cup shredded fresh sage leaves
1-2 tablespoons unsalted butter (optional)
5 cups cubed stale sourdough bread
¼ cup chopped flat-leaf parsley
1 capon, about 7 to 8 pounds, washed and patted dry

1. In a medium saucepan over high heat, bring water to a boil. Add 1 teaspoon salt. Add rice; return to a boil. Reduce heat to low, cover tightly, and cook for 45 minutes, or until tender. Spread on a plate to cool.
2. Meanwhile, place pancetta in a large, deep frying pan over medium-low heat. Cook until fat is rendered and pancetta is crisp, 10 to 15 minutes. Add onions and cook until they begin to soften, 2 to 3 minutes. Turn heat to medium; add carrots and celery. Cook until soft, 5 to 10 minutes. Season to taste.
3. Add stock and bring to a simmer. Add sage and reduce until thick and soupy, about 5 minutes over medium-high heat. Add butter, if desired, and stir until melted.
4. Add rice to pan and stir until moistened. Place bread cubes in a large bowl and combine with rice-vegetable mixture. Add more stock as needed until stuffing is slightly moist but not soggy. Stir in parsley.
5. Heat oven to 425°. Season cavity of capon with salt and pepper. Stuff just before roasting. Rub capon with a little softened butter or olive oil and sprinkle with salt and pepper. Tie legs together with butcher's twine and place in a roasting pan.
6. Turn oven down to 375° and roast capon for 25 minutes per pound, or until juices run clear when thigh is pricked with a fork. Let sit, loosely covered with foil, for 10 minutes before carving.
NOTE: Pancetta (cured Italian bacon) can be purchased in an Italian delicatessen or specialty store. If pancetta is unavailable, substitute regular bacon.

CHOOSING A TREE

Picking the "right" tree is a Christmas ritual in many households. There are aesthetic considerations: short-needle partisans think ornaments look best on a sparsely foliaged tree such as the Douglas fir, others prefer the fullness of a long-needled Scotch pine. But there are also practical considerations: beautiful as the spruces are, they are quickest to dry out and shed. A fir is a better choice.

Choose the tree as you would choose fruit or vegetables: the fresher the better. Visit a tree farm and cut your own; as a second choice, buy from a farm stand. When you get the tree home, cut an inch off the trunk and place it in a large bucket of water overnight. Erect the tree in the coolest corner of the room, in a sturdy stand. (If there are likely to be children or pets in the house, screw a small cup hook into the ceiling above, and secure the top of the tree to it with fine nylon fishing line.)

When it comes to disposal, many towns have recycling stations to turn trees into mulch. Alternately, one can remove the branches to use as winter mulch for perennials and shrubs. Never burn the tree: the oily soot adheres to the inside of a chimney and may catch fire.

OPPOSITE, TOP: Roast capon on a bed of roasted vegetables; BOTTOM: Christmas balls and mercury-glass globes rest in nests of bay leaves.

Wild-mushroom-and-leek beggar's purses, tied with leek ribbons and garnished with thyme, look like tiny gifts. Made ahead of time and baked at the last minute, they nicely complement both red meat and fowl.

Dainty Seckel pears were poached in white wine, then enrobed in caramel sauce just before serving. They are delicious with gingerbread and small enough to tempt even a sated appetite.

Wild Mushroom and Leek Beggar's Purses

MAKES 8

Any combination of wild mushrooms can be used; try chanterelles and shiitakes.

4   leeks, washed thoroughly
4   tablespoons olive oil
1½   pounds wild mushrooms, cleaned and sliced or left
        whole, depending on size
1-2   tablespoons fresh thyme leaves
        Salt and freshly ground pepper
¼   cup Madeira or veal or beef stock
6   sheets frozen phyllo dough, thawed in refrigerator
6-8   tablespoons unsalted butter, melted

1. Split leeks in half lengthwise, leaving root attached. Remove some of the inner layers to use for tying purses; blanch them for 30 seconds in boiling water, refresh in cool water, drain, and set aside.
2. Remove green tops and thinly slice leeks. Sauté in 1 tablespoon of the oil until soft, about 5 minutes. Do not brown. Remove from pan to a large bowl.
3. Add another tablespoon of oil to pan, turn heat to medium high, and add enough mushrooms to cover bottom of pan. Cook, stirring frequently, until just softened, about 3 minutes. Remove from pan and add to leeks. Repeat until all mushrooms are cooked. If using a variety of mushrooms, cook each type separately.
4. Return mushrooms and leeks to pan. Add thyme, salt, pepper, and Madeira or stock, and cook over high heat, stirring, until liquid is reduced to a syrupy consistency. Set aside to cool.
5. Unwrap phyllo pastry and unroll flat. Cover completely with damp dish towel to prevent drying out. Lay out a sheet of phyllo and brush it sparingly with melted butter. Repeat until you have three layers. Cut into 4 rectangles. Place ⅓ cup filling in the center of each and gather into a cinched-purse shape. Repeat with remaining filling. (Wrap and refreeze remaining phyllo dough.) Chill purses until firm.
6. Heat oven to 400°. Place purses on a baking sheet and bake until evenly golden brown, about 15 minutes. Tie each purse with a leek ribbon and serve hot.

ABOVE RIGHT: Fig branches and iridescent organdy ribbon are draped around a chandelier. OPPOSITE: Tiny cakes of warm gingerbread are served with whipped cream and a sliver of candied ginger.

Caramel Coated Seckel Pears

SERVES 8

The pears must be poached at least a day ahead of serving.

1   bottle dry white wine
3   cups sugar
1   lemon, cut in half
1   cinnamon stick
        Several cloves
        Several peppercorns
16   Seckel pears
½   cup water

1. Combine wine, 1 cup of the sugar, 1 lemon half, and the spices in a medium saucepan. Bring mixture to a boil; simmer for 10 minutes.
2. Peel pears carefully, retaining stems. Sprinkle with juice from remaining lemon half. Add pears to poaching liquid and bring to a bare simmer.
3. Cover pears with a lid slightly smaller than the pot to keep them submerged. Cook for 10 to 30 minutes, depending on size and ripeness of pears, or until tender and translucent. Rearrange pears once or twice to ensure even cooking. Cool pears in poaching liquid; refrigerate overnight.

4. Remove pears from liquid, discarding liquid, and drain on paper towels. Dry pears as much as possible and set aside. Combine remaining 2 cups sugar and the water in a medium, heavy saucepan over low heat. Stir occasionally, until sugar dissolves. Cover pan and bring to a boil. Leave cover on until condensation washes down the insides of the pan. Set a large pan of cold water near stove. Turn heat to medium high and boil syrup, without stirring, until it becomes a deep amber. Carefully plunge bottom of pot into pan of cold water to stop the cooking.

5. Holding each pear by the stem, carefully dip in hot caramel and set on a lightly oiled baking sheet. When pears have been dipped, drizzle remaining caramel over tops. Let cool; serve within 30 minutes.

Gingerbread

MAKES ONE 9-BY-13-INCH CAKE OR 16 INDIVIDUAL CAKES

Quite different from the gingerbread of cookies and Hansel-and-Gretel houses, this is old-fashioned, spicy gingerbread cake.

1	cup boiling water
2	teaspoons baking soda
2½	cups all-purpose flour
2	teaspoons ground ginger
1½	teaspoons ground cinnamon
½	teaspoon ground cloves
2	teaspoons baking powder
8	tablespoons (1 stick) unsalted butter
¾	cup dark brown sugar
1	cup unsulfured molasses
2	large eggs, lightly beaten
	Confectioners' sugar, for dusting
	Whipped cream, for garnish
	Candied Ginger (recipe follows)

1. Preheat oven to 350°. Butter a 9-by-13-inch pan or sixteen 3-inch oval molds and set aside. Combine water with baking soda. Set aside. In a large bowl, sift together flour, spices, and baking powder. Set aside.

2. In another large bowl, cream butter. Add sugar and beat until fluffy. Beat in molasses and baking-soda mixture. Beat in flour mixture. Add eggs and beat well.

3. Pour batter into pan and bake for 35 minutes (a toothpick inserted into center should come out clean). Cool on wire rack. To serve, dust with confectioners' sugar and top with whipped cream and a slice of Candied Ginger.

Candied Ginger

MAKES ¼ CUP

We used the ginger as a garnish for our gingerbread; it can also be served alone at the end of a meal.

1	3-inch knob fresh ginger
1	cup sugar, plus more for rolling
1	cup water

1. Peel ginger and cut into paper-thin slices, using a vegetable peeler.

2. Combine sugar and water in a small saucepan over medium heat and bring to a boil. Cook until sugar dissolves, about 5 minutes. Add ginger slices; simmer over low heat until translucent, 15 to 20 minutes.

3. Drain candied ginger slices in a colander; roll each piece in sugar. Ginger can be candied several days ahead and stored in an airtight container.

Apple Charlotte

SERVES 8

If you do not have a charlotte mold, any round, flat-bottomed two-quart casserole can be used in its place.

11	tablespoons unsalted butter, softened
6	pounds tart apples such as McIntosh or Gravenstein, peeled, cored, and thinly sliced
2	tablespoons fresh lemon juice
1	vanilla bean, split and scraped
¾	cup sugar
3	tablespoons brandy or Calvados (optional)
1	loaf thin-sliced white bread or brioche
1	cup heavy cream, whipped if desired

1. Melt 4 tablespoons of the butter in a large saucepan over medium-low heat. Add apple slices, lemon juice, vanilla bean and scrapings, sugar, and brandy or Calvados, if desired. Cook until apples break down and become a chunky applesauce, about 20 minutes. Continue cooking, uncovered, over low heat until mixture is stiff enough to hold its shape when you press a spoon into it, 10 to 15 minutes longer. Remove and discard vanilla bean. Let sauce cool and refrigerate until cold (see Note).

2. Heat oven to 400°. Trim crusts from bread and discard. Place 4 slices of bread together in a square, and place a 7-inch charlotte mold on top. Trace shape of mold onto bread with knife tip, and cut it to fit in bottom of mold. Butter on both sides and fit into mold.

3. Reserve at least 4 slices of bread for the top; cut remaining slices in half lengthwise. They should about the same height as the mold. Butter rectangles on both sides and fit them against walls of mold, overlapping like shingles. Fill with apple mixture. Cut reserved bread to fit top of mold; butter, and fit into place. Chill 15 minutes.

4. Bake until bread is golden brown, 30 to 40 minutes. Let cool in pan for at least 30 minutes. Unmold and serve warm with heavy cream, whipped if desired.

NOTE: The applesauce can be prepared several days before the charlotte is to be assembled and baked.

ABOVE LEFT: **A pale-green Venetian glass goblet takes its place in the eclectic table setting.** LEFT: **The apple charlotte, raised on a low cake pedestal and garnished with a loose bow of organdy ribbon.** OPPOSITE: **At the end of a festive meal, an array of individual desserts is especially tempting. Our buffet held poached pears, gingerbread, cranberry linzer tarts, and an apple charlotte.**

Cranberry Linzer Tarts

MAKES ONE 9-INCH OR EIGHT 3-INCH TARTS

Linzer torte is a traditional Austrian dessert with a fruit-preserve filling; whole fruit gives it a bit more body. The filling can be made two days ahead of time.

4	cups fresh cranberries
1	cup dried cranberries
1	cup sugar
	Grated zest of 1 orange
½	cup water
1	recipe Linzer Dough (recipe follows)

1. Combine cranberries, sugar, zest, and water in a medium saucepan. Bring to a boil; lower heat and simmer until fresh cranberries begin to burst, about 10 minutes.
2. Remove cranberries with a slotted spoon to a bowl, leaving liquid in the pan. Reduce liquid over low heat until thick, about 10 minutes. Pour over cranberries and mix well. Set aside to cool.

3. Roll out dough to ⅛ inch thick. Line a 9-inch tart pan or eight 3-inch tart pans with dough. Chill until firm, about 30 minutes. Roll out remaining dough to make lattice or leaves to decorate top. Chill on a baking sheet until firm.
4. Heat oven to 375°. Fill tart shells and decorate tops, attaching lattice or leaves with a bit of ice water. Bake until pastry is brown and filling is bubbling around edges, about 30 minutes.

LINZER DOUGH

½	pound whole blanched almonds
2	cups all-purpose flour
⅓	cup sugar
	Pinch of salt
	Pinch of ground cloves
½	teaspoon ground cinnamon
1	tablespoon grated orange zest
½	pound (2 sticks) cold unsalted butter, cut into ½-inch pieces
4	large egg yolks
2	teaspoons ice water
½	teaspoon almond or vanilla extract

1. Heat oven to 325°. Spread almonds on a baking sheet and toast 8 to 10 minutes, shaking pan occasionally; do not brown. Let cool. Finely grind in a spice grinder. You will have about a cup.
2. Combine almonds, flour, sugar, salt, spices, and zest in a food processor. Add butter and process with short pulses until mixture resembles coarse meal.
3. In a small bowl, combine egg yolks, ice water, and extract. With machine running, add yolk mixture to processor. Process for no longer than 30 seconds. If mixture does not hold together when squeezed, add additional water, a few teaspoons at a time, until it does.
4. Wrap in plastic and chill about 1 hour.

NOTE: The dough makes enough for one 9-inch tart shell or eight 3-inch tarts, and can be frozen, well wrapped, for up to 2 weeks before using.

ABOVE LEFT: A wreath of fresh bay leaves decorates an entry hall.

OPPOSITE, RIGHT: Cranberry linzer tarts, an Austrian dessert turned American; FAR RIGHT: Tiffany's Audubon silverware, designed in 1871.

FINISHING TOUCHES

When planning a festive dinner, one is tempted to end with a pièce de résistance: the flaming plum pudding, the elaborately decorated cake. Guests can be overwhelmed, rather than tempted, as a result. We prefer to present an array of desserts, some rich, some light, with as many as possible made in individual servings. Tartlets replace pies; gingerbread is baked in tiny cakes; custards are served in ramekins. Some desserts—charlotte, for example—do not lend themselves to this treatment, but most do. We have enjoyed experimenting with favorite sweets, and have amassed a great collection of tartlet molds and custard cups in the process.

Dried pomegranates, limes, and a sycamore ball dressed for the holidays in crinkle wire, ribbons, and gold twine. Any mix of dried fruit and trim will brighten the tree.

We have made Christmas ornaments from gilded nuts, from dried leaves, from shells, and from popcorn. One year, we were inspired by memories of the orange tucked into the toe of a Christmas stocking to make ornaments from dried fruit. The ribbon-wrapped orange, above, was made as follows: Wrap a band of satin ribbon around a dried orange, securing ends with a hot-glue gun. Repeat with a narrower band of ribbon, then with a piece of crinkled wire. With the hot-glue gun, attach a minute brass "eye" to the stem end of the orange, and thread with a loop of cord.

We recommend using commercially dried fruit to make the ornaments on these pages; drying fruit at home can take several months and yield uneven results. Freeze-dried fruit, though more expensive than air-dried, retains its color better. The lemon, above, is freeze-dried while the orange to the left has been air-dried. To decorate the banded lemon, glue adjacent bands of red and green satin ribbon around lemon. Cover gap with gold ribbon. Press four upholstery tacks at intervals through ribbons. To make a tassel, glue a short length of gold twine to tip of lemon, fraying its end. Coat lemon tip with glue and wrap with gold twine. Over a small "x" of red and green ribbon, attach a brass hook to stem end.

The lightness of dried fruit makes it ideal for hanging on the holiday tree, and since the shapes have been designed by nature for tree decoration, they often need little embellishment. We covered pomegranates, limes, and sycamore balls with strands of simple crinkled wire. To hang the pomegranates and lime, press an upholstery tack into each end, wrap stem end with gold twine, and make loop. For the sycamore ball, glue twine to base of stem and wrap stem, ending in a knotted loop.

LEAFY ORANGE (left): Make a short loop of satin ribbon, attaching it to one end of orange with a brass upholstery tack, slightly raised. Wrap a four-inch length of fine-gauge gold wire a few times around the stems of two molded-brass-mesh leaves. Wrap wire around tack and press tack in. Finish with a tack at other end of orange. **GOLD-LEAF WREATH** (opposite): Wrap a ten-inch double flat metal wreath form with gold-mesh ribbon, gluing loose end to form. Make a wire stem for each of one hundred molded-brass-mesh leaves

by doubling a ten-inch length of fine-gauge gold wire and winding one end a few times around leaf's stem. Twist six to eight leaves together at stems to form a flat cluster, as shown above; repeat with remaining leaves. Twist bunches onto a length of florist's wire equal to the wreath form's circumference. Lay garland on form, leaves facing up. Bind garland to form with gold wire. Curl leaves by hand. Finish with an organdy bow.

New Year's Eve

TIME WAS, WE SPENT THE LAST NIGHT OF THE YEAR *at a raucous party. Then children and reality arrived, and we learned that finding a New Year's Eve babysitter was akin to winning the lottery. So we gathered best friends for small suppers at home and toasted at midnight while babies dozed in corners about the house. Now some of those babies have houses and babies of their own, but*

New Year's Eve at home has become a pleasant ritual. Over a simple but elegant meal, we review the year just past. We make our annual resolutions (yes, they are the same every year). Mostly, we take stock of our lives; as we grow older, we find ourselves giving ever greater thanks for our companions. As Thanksgiving and Christmas are times for family, New Year's Eve is time for our friends.

MENU

Beef Broth with Pasta Stars

Galette of Root Vegetables

Stuffed Lamb Chops

Chiffonade of Kale

Black-Currant Ice Cream in Brandy Snap Cups

OPPOSITE: **A star-stenciled tablecloth, huge mercury-glass witches' balls, and rosemary topiaries spangled with tiny white lights decorate an enclosed porch for a late-night supper. (The star shapes left over after we cut the card for the stencils were so pretty we painted them silver and hung them on the house plants.)**

PHOTOGRAPHS BY JON JENSEN

Beef Broth with Pasta Stars

SERVES 8

*If time is short, commercial "fresh" pasta can be
substituted for the homemade version. Do not substitute canned
broth, however; the result would be disappointing.*

4	tablespoons vegetable oil
2	pounds beef ribs
2	pounds veal shank
2	pounds beef bones
2	onions, unpeeled
4	carrots, unpeeled
4	celery stalks, with leaves
2	cloves garlic, unpeeled
1	small bunch parsley
3	sprigs fresh thyme
2	bay leaves
	Salt and freshly ground pepper
	Chopped fresh chives, for garnish

1. Heat oven to 350°.

2. Heat oil in a heavy roasting pan and add beef, veal, bones,
vegetables, and garlic. Place pan in oven and allow contents
to brown for 1 to 2 hours. Do not allow to burn.

3. Remove pan from oven and add enough water to cover
contents. Add parsley, thyme, and bay leaves. Simmer, uncovered, on to of stove for 4 to 5 hours. Do not boil, season, or
stir, or broth will become cloudy.

4. Strain broth, discarding bones and vegetables. Chill broth;
remove all fat from surface. Return broth to simmer; strain
through fine cheesecloth. Season to taste with salt and pepper.

5. Just before serving, add cooked Red Pepper Pasta and Basil
Pasta (recipes follow) to broth. Garnish with chopped chives.

RED PEPPER PASTA

2	red bell peppers, roasted, peeled, and seeded (page 16)
½	teaspoon hot-red-pepper flakes
1	tablespoon olive oil
1	teaspoon salt
2	large eggs
2	egg yolks
3½	cups all-purpose flour

1. Combine peppers, hot-pepper flakes, olive oil, salt, eggs,
egg yolks, and flour in a food processor. Process until smooth.
Dough will gather into a ball.

2. Using a pasta machine and following manufacturer's directions, roll dough into wide strips. Cut into shapes. Wrap and chill until ready to use.

BASIL PASTA

⅓ cup finely chopped fresh basil
1 teaspoon salt
1 tablespoon olive oil
3½ cups all-purpose flour
4-5 large eggs

1. Combine basil, salt, olive oil, and flour in a food processor. Blend in 4 of the eggs, adding the fifth if dough seems a little too dry. Process until smooth. Dough will gather into a ball.
2. Follow directions above for rolling, cutting, and storing.

Galette of Root Vegetables

SERVES 8

A variation on the traditional French potato galette, this vegetable "pancake" can be made with almost any combination of roots.

2 carrots, peeled
2 white turnips, peeled
1 parsnip, peeled
3 large Idaho potatoes, peeled
8 tablespoons (1 stick) unsalted butter, clarified
   Salt and freshly ground pepper

1. Coarsely grate all vegetables, using a mandoline if possible. Dry grated potatoes by rubbing them between cloth towels.
2. Heat the clarified butter in a 12-inch nonstick skillet until it sizzles. Mix together grated vegetables and place in skillet in a flat, even layer. Sprinkle with salt and pepper. Cook over medium-high heat, shaking pan gently to prevent sticking.
3. After about 10 minutes, invert the vegetables onto a plate (the underside of the galette should be golden brown) and slide them back into the pan to continue cooking on the other side. Reduce heat to low and cook for another 20 to 30 minutes, shaking pan from time to time.
4. Serve warm, cut into wedges.

TOP LEFT: Uncooked, fresh pasta can be shaped with a cookie cutter or sharp knife. BOTTOM LEFT: Vintage silver plate chargers and a mix of antique flatware patterns combine to set a magical table.

A STENCILED TABLECLOTH

To create your own stencil, trace designs onto firm card and cut out. If using a precut stencil, press out perforations and trim inside edges with a sharp blade. Lay clean, ironed fabric on a hard, flat surface. Spray the back of stencil with spray mount and position on fabric. Dip stencil brush lightly into fabric paint and daub over stencil, keeping the brush perpendicular. Remove the stencil carefully, reposition it, and repeat the process. Once the design is complete, let paint dry and iron fabric on back to set. (We made our hollow-centered stars by placing a penny in the middle of design.)

Stuffed lamb chops tied with a leek ribbon and surrounded by vegetable galette and acorn squash filled with kale. Opposite: Simple steps—cutting, grating, chopping, rolling—to a glorious meal.

Stuffed Lamb Chops

SERVES 8

*This recipe calls for boning lamb chops; if time is short,
boned chops can be ordered from a good butcher.*

8 double-thick loin lamb chops
4 tablespoons (½ stick) unsalted butter
1 leek, cleaned and julienned
2 red peppers, seeded and julienned
3 cloves garlic, peeled and minced
½ cup white-bread crumbs
4 sprigs fresh rosemary, stemmed and chopped
12 sprigs fresh thyme, 4 of them stemmed and chopped
   Salt and freshly ground pepper
3 tablespoons olive oil
2 extra leeks, whole

1. Remove the bone and all of the fat from each lamb chop.
2. Melt butter in a skillet and sauté julienned leek, red peppers, and garlic until just tender. Add bread crumbs, chopped
rosemary, and chopped thyme. Season with salt and pepper.
Reduce heat and continue to cook for 5 minutes.
3. Spoon stuffing onto each lamb chop. Roll each chop tightly
and tie with butcher's twine. Heat olive oil in a skillet until it
sizzles. Brown chops with thyme sprigs, salt, and pepper.
4. Meanwhile, bring a large pot of water to a boil. Carefully
separate the leaves of the whole leeks and wash off all dirt.
Blanch for 20 to 30 seconds, plunge into ice water ,and drain.
5. Heat oven to 350°.
6. Remove chops from skillet and let cool slightly. Wrap one
leek "ribbon" around each chop and tie with a bow.
7. Place chops in baking dish with a small amount of olive oil
and bake for 12 to 15 minutes; serve immediately.
NOTE: This dish can be prepared ahead of time until step 7.

Boning a lamb chop is easy if you have the right tool (a really sharp
knife) and the right material: a double-thick loin chop. Cut out the
bone, keeping as close to it as possible. Remove all the fat, and
flatten the chop to prepare it for stuffing. Once the technique is
mastered, it can be adapted to other kinds of chops and stuffings.
The rolled and tied chop makes a neat package on the plate.

Chiffonade of Kale

SERVES 8

"Chiffonade" means leaves cut into very fine strips.

4 cloves garlic, minced
4 cloves garlic, peeled and minced
1 pound fresh kale, cut into a very fine chiffonade
   Salt and freshly ground pepper

In a large skillet, sauté the garlic in olive oil for 5 minutes.
Add kale, sauté for 5 minutes, season, and serve immediately.

Brandy Snap Cups

MAKES 10 CUPS

Brandy snaps are traditionally formed into tubes (wrap around buttered wooden-spoon handles right after they emerge from oven). For this dessert, we formed them into cups: you'll need three glass ramekins or custard cups about four and a half inches in diameter and two inches deep.

8   tablespoons (1 stick) unsalted butter
½   cup sugar
⅓   cup molasses
¼   teaspoon ground ginger
½   teaspoon ground cinnamon
1   teaspoon grated orange rind
½   cup all-purpose flour
2   tablespoons cognac

1. Combine butter, sugar, molasses, spices, and orange rind in a saucepan and bring to a boil. Remove from the heat and stir in the flour, using a wire whisk. Add the cognac and stir, blending until mixture is smooth.
2. Heat oven to 350°.
3. Drop mixture, ¼ cup at a time, onto parchment-covered baking sheets. Space widely. Prepare only three snaps at a time; they harden quickly once removed from the oven and are difficult to shape.
4. Bake for 10 to 12 minutes. Remove and let cool for a minute or so. Run a thin spatula around the perimeter of one snap at a time to loosen bottom completely. Quickly place snap inside one of the ramekins to mold into a cup shape. Let cool. (If the snaps become hard before removing from baking sheet, return briefly to oven to soften.)

CARAMEL SAUCE

MAKES ABOUT 2 CUPS

1   cup sugar
¼   cup water
1   cup heavy cream
1   teaspoon vanilla extract

In a heavy pot, preferably a copper sugar pot, melt sugar with the water over high heat. Do not stir mixture or caramel will cloud; swirl pot gently instead. Boil until sugar becomes the color of maple syrup. Do not allow to burn. Remove from heat and whisk in the heavy cream. Add vanilla. Let sauce cool; store in refrigerator until ready to use.

Black Currant Ice Cream

SERVES 8

We grow black currants in the garden; at summer's end, we cook them with a little water, puree, sieve, and freeze. Frozen currants can be found in specialty stores and similarly pureed.

1¼   cups heavy cream
⅔   cup half-and-half
3   large egg yolks
½   cup sugar
6   tablespoons black-currant puree

1. Heat cream and half-and-half in a stainless-steel saucepan. Beat yolks and sugar together. Slowly add cream to egg mixture, whisking constantly. Return mixture to saucepan and reheat very gently; do not allow to boil. Stir with a wooden spoon until mixture thickens and coats back of spoon. Remove from heat and strain. Stir in black-currant puree.
2. Place a piece of plastic wrap or parchment directly on top of custard to prevent skin from forming; chill custard completely. Pour into an ice-cream maker and freeze according to manufacturer's instructions.

SPUN SUGAR

Spinning sugar is easy, and the effects are astonishing. For the best results, you'll need a wooden laundry rack placed on a newspaper-covered floor, and a wire balloon whisk with the rounded end cut off to form "tines."

2   cups sugar
⅔   cup water
2   tablespoons corn syrup

1. Bring sugar, water, and corn syrup to a boil over high heat. Do not stir. Cover pan until steam dissolves any crystals. Uncover and boil 5 minutes or longer until syrup is amber. Remove from heat; plunge base of pot into cold water.
2. Dip the tines of the whisk into syrup and gently toss back and forth across laundry rack. Syrup will harden on contact with the air and will form translucent strands. When syrup is used up, pick up strands of spun sugar and form into nests around Black-Currant Ice Cream.

RIGHT: Dessert, wrapped with a cloud of spun sugar, is served on vintage silver-luster plates set atop silver-plate chargers. Glasses found at a tag sale hold champagne for toasting the New Year.

The Photographers

WILLIAM ABRANOWICZ
contents (middle right), pages 45 (left), 66, 67.

ANTOINE BOOTZ
contents (top left), pages 14, 16-18, 20, 21, 70-72, 74-89.

JOHN DUGDALE
contents (top and bottom right),
dedication page, introduction,
pages 15, 24-37, 44, 45 (right), 48-59, 67, 68, 139,143.

TODD EBERLE
contents (middle left), pages 90-93, 94 (top right), 96-101.

JON JENSEN
pages 122-127, 129.

VICTORIA PEARSON
contents (bottom left),
acknowledgments, pages 38-41, 60, 61, 64, 102-121, 131.

JERRY SIMPSON
page 45 (middle).

MARIA ROBLEDO
pages 42, 43, 46.

ELIZABETH ZESCHIN
pages 62, 63, 64 (bottom left and right), 65, 94, 95.

The Guide

PLEASE NOTE:
Items pictured but not listed are from private collections. Addresses and telephone numbers of sources may change prior to publication, as may price and availability of any item.

THANKSGIVING DINNER
Recipes *from Ina Garten, The Barefoot Contessa, 46 Newtown Lane, East Hampton, NY 11937, 516-324-0240.*
Dessert recipes *from Kathleen's Bake Shop Cookbook, St. Martin's Press.*

PAGES 14 AND 21
Handpainted China Trade **mural**, $3,800, *from Wendy Stone, The Garden Studio, 207 Mill Road, New Canaan, CT 06880, 203-966-9072.*

PAGES 15, 24, 25
Atlantic Giant **pumpkin seeds** *from Howard Dill Enterprises, 400 College Road, Windsor, Nova Scotia, Canada B0N 2T0, 902-798-2728.*

PAGES 16, 20
Game birds *from D'Artagnan, 399 St. Paul's Avenue, Jersey City, NJ 07306, 201-792-0748; Griggstown Quail Farm Inc., R.D. 1, Canal Road, Princeton, NJ 08540, 201-359-5375; Pintelle (for French-bred Pintelle guinea hens only), 424 Yonge Street, Suite 808, Toronto, Ontario, Canada M5B 2H3, 416-597-0516.*

PERFECT PIES
Special thanks to Laura Plimpton for her pie-tin collection.

PAGE 28
Wooden **pie rack**, $95, *from Pat Guthman Antiques, 281 Pequot Avenue, Southport, CT 06490, 203-259-5743.*

PAGE 29
Georgian silver **fork**, $100, *from I. Freeman & Son Inc., 60 East 56th Street, New York, NY 10022, 212-759-6900.*

PAGE 30
Antique bird's-eye-maple **rolling pin**, $200, *at Vito Giallo Antiques, 966 Madison Avenue, New York, NY 10021, 212-535-9885.*
Curly maple rolling pin (circa 1800), from $60, *from Pat Guthman Antiques, 281 Pequot Avenue, Southport, CT 06490, 203-259-5743.*

PAGE 31
Small **pie tins**, $65, *from Linda Cheverton Art & Antiques, Box 53, Colebrook, CT 06021, 203-379-5345.*
French antique handwoven linen **towel**, $40, *at Trouvaille Française, 212-737-6015 (by appointment only).*

PAGE 33
Ironstone dessert **plate**, $50, *from Vito Giallo Antiques, 966 Madison Avenue, New York, NY 10021, 212-535-9885.*

PAGE 34
Fluted **pie tin**, $75, *from Linda Cheverton Art & Antiques, Box 53, Colebrook, CT 06021, 203-379-5345.*

PAGE 35
Sterling-handled **pie server**, $100; Victorian silver-plated **trowel** with ivory handle, $350; sterling-handled **repoussé pie server**, $100; *all from I. Freeman & Son Inc., 60 East 56th Street, New York, NY 10022, 212-759-6900.*
Sterling pie server, $75; **mother-of-pearl-handled pie server**, $75, *both from Vito Giallo Antiques, 966 Madison Avenue, New York, NY 10021, 212-535-9885.*

PAGE 37
French antique octagonal Creil **plates**, $50 each, *from Pierre Deux Antiques, 369 Bleecker Street, New York, NY 10014, 212-243-7740.*

PAGES 38, 39, 40, 41
Apples (thirty-five varieties) and homemade preserves and chutneys *from Peter Zimmermann and Elizabeth Ryan, Breezy Hill Orchard, 200 Centre Road, Staatsburg, NY 12580, 914-266-5967. Mail order available.*

Antique trees (more than one hundred varieties grafted onto a wide selection of rootstock), apple-tasting sampler packs, and custom grafting, *from Sonoma Antique Apple Nursery, 4395 Westside Road, Healdsburg, CA 95448, 707-433-6420.*
Apple trees (forty selections grafted onto a wide selection of rootstock) *from Ed Fackler, Rocky Meadow Orchard and Nursery, 360 Rocky Meadow Road NW, New Salisbury, IN 47161, 812-347 2213. Catalog, $1.*
Apple trees (two hundred varieties, including single trees bearing two to four varieties on five selections of rootstock) *from South Meadow Fruit Farm, 15310 Red Arrow Highway, Lakeside, MI 49116, 616-4696-2865. Mail order available.*
Apple-scion listings *from Seed Savers Yearbook, Seed Savers Exchange, RR3, Box 239, Decorah, IA 52101. Membership, $25 per year.*

HOMEMADE GIFTS

PAGE 42
Seasonal **citrus fruits** available by mail order *from Lang Sun Country Groves,*

5900 Highways 17 and 92, Lake Alfred, FL 33850, 813-956-1460. Also from Policicchio Groves, 800-452-4866.
Tissue paper by Crystal Tissue Paper Co., *available at stationery stores nationwide.*

PAGE 43
Two-inch-wide pleated-velvet **ribbon,** $17 per yard, *from Bell'occhio, 8 Brady Street, San Francisco, CA 94103, 415-864-4048.*
Shaker boxes by Green Mountain Studios, *available at craft stores nationwide.* Livos **stain paste,** $7.25 for .125 liter; Livos Kaldet **resin-and-oil finish,** $17.95 for .75 liter; Livos Vindo **enamel paint,** $8.25 for .125 liter; *all from Terra Verde, 72 Spring Street, New York, NY 10012, 212-925-4533.*

PAGE 44
Sweetser half-peck **basket** with swing-back handle, $75, *from Brown Ash Basketry, Box 183, Franconia, NH 03580, 603-823-8161. Brochure $1.*
Set of six assorted Spanish **bottles,** $32, and pop-up **sponges,** $7.50 and $9, *from Williams-Sonoma Inc., 800-541-2233.*
Swedish **vegetable peeler,** set

of two $8.50; **rubber grip,** set of four $11; **dish brush,** $2.50; **heat diffuser,** $3.50; stainless-steel **spoon rest,** $3.50; **pie spatula,** $2.75; flexible stainless **spatula,** $3.50; orangewood **toothpicks,** $3.95; **knife,** $7.75, *all from from The Vermont Country Store, Box 3000, Manchester Center, VT 05255, 802-362-2400.*
Ruffled **clamshells,** $4, *from Blooming Shells, Main Street, Sag Harbor, NY 11963, 516-725-4428.*
Wax blocks, $2.33 per pound; Number 2 **wicking,** $2.40 per yard (ten-yard minimum); *both from Dadant & Sons, 800-443-8738.*
Fortnum & Mason Fortmason Blend **tea,** 250-gram tin $16.95, *from Myers of Keswick English Specialty Foods, 634 Hudson Street, New York, NY 10014, 212-691-4194.*
Le Blomvilliers **brown sugar,** one-kilogram box $5.80; yellow rock **crystal sugar,** $5.50 per pound, *from Dean & Deluca Inc., 212-431-1691 or (outside New York) 800-221-7714 extensions 223 or 270.*
Tiffany sterling **tea ball,** $700, *from I. Freeman & Son, Inc., 60 East 56th*

Street, New York, NY 10022, 212-759-6900.
Metallic **tissue paper** by The Crystal Tissue Co., *at paper, art, and department stores nationwide.*
Two and a quarter inch wide **metallic ribbon,** $8 per yard, *from Brimar Inc., 1706 Marcee Lane, Box 2621, Northbrook, IL 60065, 708-272-9585.*

PAGE 45
Set of six assorted Spanish **bottles,** $32; set of six 16-ounce **grape-pattern bottles,** $21, *from Williams-Sonoma Inc., 800-541-2233.*
Lustregild **copper enamel,** one-quarter pint $4.50 plus $2 for shipping, *from Absolute Coatings Inc., 34 Industrial Street, Bronx, NY 10461, 212-892-1800.*
Twenty-one-by-thirty-six-inch **dog bed,** $39.99; slicker **brush,** $8.49; **flea comb,** $5.99; **Boomer ball,** $19.99; Tuffy **chew toy,** $3.99; Booda **tug toy,** $6.99; **Pet Tabs,** $11.89; **liver treats,** $4.95; steel **bowls,** $2.45-$3.55; Gumabone **frisbee,** $5.95, *all from Econo-Vet, 8687 Blumenstein Road, Box 1191, Minocqua, WI 54548, 715-369-5591 or (outside Wisconsin) 800-451-4162.*
Leather **leash,** $14.98;

squeaky toy, $4.99; **rawhide bone**, $5.99, *all from Calling All Pets, 301 East 76th Street, New York, NY 10021, 212-249-7387. Mother Knows Best: The Natural Way to Train Your Dog by Carol Lea Benjamin, $18.95 (Howell Book House Publishers), at bookstores nationwide*

PAGE 46

Five-eighths-inch-wide satin **ribbon**, $1.30 per yard, *from Hyman Hendler & Sons, 67 West 38th Street, New York, NY 10018, 212-840-8393. Minimum mail order $20.*

AFTERNOON TEA

PAGE 48

Black and white **transferware teapot**, $165; **stand**, $60; **Worcester teapot**, $210, *all from Charterhouse Antiques Ltd., 115 Greenwich Avenue, New York, NY 10014, 212-243-4726.*

Ridgway **porcelain teapot and stand**, $935 *from James II Galleries Ltd., 15 East 57th floor, New York, NY 10022, 212-355-7040.*

Lusterware teapot, $150, *from Jenkinstown Antiques, 520 Route 32 South,*

New Paltz, NY 12561, 914-255-8135. Brownfield brown-and-white **ironstone transferware**, $500 for service for ten, *from Thumbprint Antiques, Stone Ridge, NY 12484, 914-687-9318.*

PAGE 49

Catskill Moss English **tea bowl with saucer**, $60, *from Charterhouse Antiques Ltd., 115 Greenwich Avenue, New York, NY 10014, 212-243-4726.*

PAGE 50

ABOVE: Early nineteenth-century wooden **tea caddy**, $535, *from James II Galleries, 15 East 57th Street, 6th floor, New York, NY 10022, 212-355-7040.* English blue-and-white earthenware **tea bowl and saucer**, $95; porcelain **tea strainer**, $15; Anderson & Tams Drury Lane Theatre **plate**, $175, *all from Charterhouse Antiques, 115 Greenwich Avenue, New York, NY 10014, 212-243-4726.*

BELOW: Cake stand, $110; coin **silver spoons**, $40 each; **purple lusterware tea bowls and saucers**, $90 each; *all from Jenkinstown Antiques, 520 Route 32 South, New Paltz, NY*

12561, 914-255-8135.

PAGE 52

ABOVE: Cake stand, $110; coin **silver spoons**, $40 each; **purple lusterware tea bowls and saucers**, $90 each; *all from Jenkinstown Antiques, 520 Route 32 South, New Paltz, NY 12561, 914-255-8135.*

BELOW: Reily and Storer silver **strainer**, $1,850; Randall Chatterton **tea-caddy spoon**, one of a $750 pair; silver **mote spoons**, from $425; Irish silver **sugar nippers**, $750; Fox's silver-gilt **tea infuser**, $2,200, *all from James Robinson, Inc., 15 East 57th Street, New York, NY 10022, 212-752-6166.* Continental **silver strainer and bowl**, $585, *from James II Galleries, 15 East 57th Street, 6th floor, New York, NY 10022, 212-355-7040.*

PAGE 53

Elkins Company Warren **plate**, $125, *from Charterhouse Antiques, 115 Greenwich Avenue, New York, NY 10014, 212-234-4726.* Antique linen **bread warmer**, $10, *from Anichini, 800-553-5309.*

PAGES 54 AND 55

Lusterware **teapot**, $150, *from Jenkinstown Antiques, 520 Route 32*

South, New Paltz, NY 12561, 914-255-8135. English Rural Scenery china **plate**, $80, *from Charterhouse Antiques, 115 Greenwich Avenue, New York, NY 10014, 212-234-4726.* Sheffield George V silver **tea infuser**, $265, *from James II Galleries, 15 East 57th Street, 6th floor, New York, NY 10022, 212-355-7040.*

PAGE 57

Brownfield brown and white ironstone **transferware**, $500 for service for 10, *from Thumbprint Antiques, Stone Ridge, NY 12484, 914-687-9318.* Perruche **brown sugar cubes**, $2.90 for seventeen-and-a-half-ounce box, *from Dean & Deluca, 212-431-1691 or (outside New York) 800-221-7714 extensions 223 or 270.* Mother-of-pearl-handled **berry spoon**, $350 for a pair; silver-plate Victorian spreader, $35; Continental silver **bowl**, $585 with strainer; *all from James II Galleries, 15 East 57th Street, 6th floor, New York, NY 10022, 212-355-7040.*

PAGE 58

English porcelain **tea bowl and saucer**, $225, *from*

James II Galleries, 15 East 57th Street, 6th floor, New York, NY 10022, 212-355-7040.

English **amethyst earthenware tea bowl and saucer,** $85; English **black-and-white transferware cup and saucer,** $45 each, *from Charterhouse Antiques, 115 Greenwich Avenue, New York, NY 10014, 212-234-4726.*

GIFT WRAPPINGS

PAGE 60

Rayon velvet child's **dress** by Mousefeathers, $160 *from selected Nordstrom stores nationwide.*

Blue-green **man's suit** by Hugo Boss, $745; ecru **man's shirt** by Giorgio Armani, $190; citrus print **tie** by Yves Saint Laurent, $82; **velvet evening shirt** by Susie Tompkins, $188; *all from I. Magnin, 135 Stockton Street, San Francisco, CA 94108, 415-362-2100.*

Necklace, $276, and **earrings,** $85 both by Subtle Creatures; vermeil **bracelet** by John Iverson, $1,895, *all from 22 Steps, 280 Sutter Street, San Francisco, CA 94108.*

PAGE 61

Chippendale-style **side chair,** $9,500 for set of eight, *from Daniel Stein Antiques, 458 Jackson Street, San Francisco, CA 94111, 415-956-5620.*

Metallic **tissue paper** by Crystal Tissue Paper Company, *at stationery stores nationwide.*

Lustregild **copper enamel,** $4.50 per quarter pint, *from Absolute Coatings, Inc., 34 Industrial Street, Bronx, NY 10461, 212-892-1800.*

Two-inch-wide luminescent organdy **ribbon,** $2-3 per yard, *from Bell'occhio, 8 Brady Street, San Francisco CA 94103; or contact Midori Inc., 3827 Stone Way North, Seattle, WA 98103, 206-547-9553 for retail information.*

PAGE 62

Alumichrome **silver enamel,** $5.20 per half-pint, *from Absolute Coatings, Inc., 34 Industrial Street, Bronx, NY 10461, 212-892-1800.*

PAGE 63

Natural **sea sponges,** $25 for set of 2, *from The Chambers Catalog, 800-334-9790.*

PAGES 64 AND 65

Tissue paper by Crystal Tissue Paper Co., *at stationery stores nationwide.*

Two-inch-wide luminescent organdy **ribbon,** $2-3 per yard, *from Bell'occhio, 8 Brady Street, San Francisco CA 94103; or contact Midori Inc., 3827 Stone Way North, Seattle, WA 98103, 206-547-9553 for retail information.*

Lustregild **copper enamel,** $4.50 per quarter pint; Lustregild **gold enamel,** $5.75 for half pint; Alumichrome **silver enamel,** $5.20 per half-pint, *from Absolute Coatings, Inc., 34 Industrial Street, Bronx, NY 10461, 212-892-1800.*

Hot-melt **glue guns,** $8 to $30, *by Stanley Parker Inc., 800-835-1027 for information.*

PAGE 66

Custom **rubber stamps,** from $24, *from American Stamp Manufacturing Co., 121 Fulton Street, New York, NY 10038, 212-227-1877.*

PAGE 67

Metallic **tissue paper** by Crystal Tissue Paper Co., *at stationery stores nationwide.*

Metallic **ink pads,** from $5.95, *by ClearSnap Inc., Department MSL, Box 98, Anacortes, WA 98221.*

Ribbons, from 66¢ per yard, by C.M. Offray & Son, Inc., *at fabric and crafts stores nationwide.*

PAGE 68

Moiré ribbon, $2.80 to $20 per yard; **grosgrain ribbon,** $1.60 to $3.75 per yard; **velvet ribbon,** $2.25 to $9 per yard; **plaid and dotted ribbons,** $1.30 to $15 per yard; **satin ribbon,** $1 to $4 per yard; **picot-edged ribbon,** $4.75 to $8.75 per yard; **plaid taffeta ribbon,** $10 to $12 per yard, minimum mail order $20; *all at Hyman Hendler and Sons, 67 West 38th Street, New York, NY 10018, 212-840-8393.*

Antique moiré **checkerboard ribbon,** $26 per yard; **ruffle-edge grosgrain ribbon,** $3 per yard; **organdy ribbon,** $5.50 to $14 per yard; **plain ribbon,** $12 to $15 per yard; **damask ribbon,** $12 per yard; **pleated-satin ribbon,** $7.50 per yard; *all at Bell'occhio, 8 Brady Street, San Francisco, CA 94103, 415-864-4048.*

PAGE 69

Ribbons, $2 to $35 per yard, minimum mail order $20, *from Hyman Hendler and Sons, 67 West 38th Street, New York, NY 10018, 212-840-8393.*

Handmade and handpainted **papers,** from $2.50 per sheet, *at Kate's Paperie, 8 West 13th Street, New*

York, NY 10013,
212-633-0570.

CLASSIC COOKIES

Gingerbread-cookie recipe *from Patti Paige, Baked Ideas, 450 Broadway, New York, NY 10003, 212-925-9097.*

PAGES 71 THROUGH 89

Moravian **cookie cutters,** from $10, *from Salem Gift and Book Store, Box 10400, Winston-Salem, NC 27108, 919-721-7355.*
Pastry bags, tubes, tips, and **paste food colorings,** *from August Thomsen Corp., 800-645-7170.*

WREATHS AND GARLANDS

PAGE 91

Fruited frame, $490, *from Green Valley Growers, 10450 Cherry Ridge Road, Sebastopol, CA 95472, 707-823-5583. Kits and custom-made wreaths also available.*
Antique **mirror,** $7,500; French sandstone **mantel,** $18,750, *both from Charles Gaylord Antiques, 2151 Powell Street, San Francisco, CA 94133, 415-392-6085.*

PAGE 93

Magnolia **tieback** with privet, about $36, *from Green Valley Growers, 10450 Cherry Ridge Road, Sebastopol, CA 95472, 707-823-5583. Kits and custom-made tiebacks also available.*

PAGE 94

TOP LEFT: Decorated grapevine **wreath** *from Pure Mädderlake, 478 Broadway, New York, NY 10013, 212-941-7770.*
TOP RIGHT: Twenty-two-inch oak-leaf **wreath,** $38, *from Green Valley Growers, 10450 Cherry Ridge Road, Sebastopol, CA 95472, 707-823-5583. Kits and custom-made wreaths also available.*
BOTTOM LEFT: Victorian **dried-flower wreath** *from Maria Jordan, Beautiful Flowers, 15 West 26th Street, New York NY 10010, 212-686-5569.*
BOTTOM LEFT: Prickly pear **wreath,** *from PaperWhite, 263 East 10th Street, New York, NY 10009, 212-477-3361.*

PAGE 96

Fresh **greenery,** $3 to $35 per bunch ($50 minimum order), *from Green Valley Growers, 10450 Cherry*

Ridge Road, Sebastopol, CA 95472, 707-823-5583.

PAGE 97

Fourteen-inch **fruited wreath,** $60, *from Green Valley Growers, 10450 Cherry Ridge Road, Sebastopol, CA 95472, 707-823-5583.*

FAMILY BREAKFAST

PAGE 98

Hand-blown **pitcher,** $900, *from Argentum, 414 Jackson Street, #101, San Francisco, CA 94111, 415-296-7757.*
English transfer-print **plate,** $160 for set of ten, *from Upstairs at Post Street at Williams-Sonoma, 150 Post Street, San Francisco, CA 94108, 415-362-6904.*
Embroidered linen **tablecloth,** $550, *from Claire's, 3615 Sacramento Street, San Francisco, CA 94118, 415-776-9352.*

PAGE 99

Mexican sterling **flatware,** $5,000 for 160-piece place setting, *from Argentum, 414 Jackson Street, #101, San Francisco, CA 94111, 415-296-7757.*
Crystal **glass** by Elsa Peretti, $22, *from Tiffany & Co.,*

800-526-0649.
Star **compote dish,** $41; by Simon Pearce, *from Gump's, 250 Post Street, San Francisco, CA 94108, 415-982-1616.*

PAGE 100

Boy's tangerine **T-shirt,** $12, *at all Brooks Brothers stores.*

PAGE 101

Damask **napkins,** $200 for twelve, *from Upstairs at Post Street at Williams-Sonoma, 150 Post Street, San Francisco, CA 94108, 415-362-6904.*
Medium **stemmed bowl,** $100, by Simon Pearce, *from Gump's, 250 Post Street, San Francisco, CA 94108, 415-982-1616.*

CHRISTMAS DINNER

Interior design *by Jeanne White, ISID, Jeanne White Interiors, 631 O'Farrell Street, Penthouse, San Francisco, CA 94109, 415-775-1729.*

PAGE 102

Mercury-glass **saltcellars,** *from J. Garvin Mecking Inc., 72 East 11th Street, New York, NY 10003, 212-677-4316 (to the trade only).*
MalMaison **charger** by

Christofle, $320, *from Gump's, 250 Post Street, San Francisco, CA 94108, 415-982-1616.*

Audubon **flatware** by Tiffany & Co., $15,000 for service for twelve, *from Argentum, 414 Jackson Street, #101, San Francisco, CA 94111, 415-296-7757.*

Art-deco **tablecloth and napkins,** *from Linda Cheverton Art & Antiques, Box 53, Colebrook, CT 06021, 203-379-5345.*

Venetian **glasses,** $195 for set of six, *from Tail of the Yak, 2632 Ashby Avenue, Berkeley, CA 94705, 510-841-9891.*

PAGE 103
Candles, from $4.25 per pair to $8 each, *from Knorr Beeswax Products, Inc., 14906 Via De La Valle, Del Mar, CA 92014, 619-755-2051.*

Iron **urns,** $595 per pair, *from Robert Domergue & Co., 560 Jackson Street, San Francisco, CA 94133, 415-781-4034.*

PAGE 105
Chippendale-style **side chairs,** $9,500 for set of eight, *from Daniel Stein Antiques, 458 Jackson Street, San Francisco, CA 94111, 415-956-5620.*

PAGE 106
Dinner **plates** by Old Sheffield, $7,500 for set of twelve, *from Argentum, 414 Jackson Street, #101, San Francisco, CA 94111, 415-296-7757.* Cotton sateen **vest** by Susie Tompkins, $98; blue-green **man's suit** by Hugo Boss, $745; ecru **shirt** by Giorgio Armani, $190; citrus-print **tie** by Yves Saint Laurent, $82; **velvet evening shirt** by Susie Tompkins, $188; *all at I. Magnin, 135 Stockton Street, San Francisco, CA 94108, 415-362-2100.* **Necklace,** $276, and **earrings,** $85, by Subtle Creatures; vermeil **bracelet** by John Iverson, $1,895, *all at 22 Steps, 280 Sutter Street, San Francisco, CA 94108, 415-398-7797.*

PAGE 107
Rayon velvet child's **dress** by Mousefeathers, $160, *from selected Nordstrom stores nationwide.* **Popover pan,** $18, *at Williams-Sonoma stores nationwide.*

PAGE 108
Fourteen-inch **bay-leaf wreath,** $38, *from Green Valley Growers, 10450 Cherry Ridge Road, Sebastopol, CA 95472, 707-823-5583.*

Mercury-glass balls by Eurodesign, $30 (small) and $50 (medium). *Call 713-464-0795 for retail information.*

Tiered **metal stand,** $175, *from Fioridella, 1920 Polk Street, San Francisco, CA 94109, 415-775-4065.*

PAGE 110
Footed silver **salver,** $350; sterling silver **straining spoon,** $775; *both from Argentum, 414 Jackson Street, #101, San Francisco, CA 94111, 415-296-7757.*

PAGE 111
Dessert **cake stands,** from $130 to $250 each, or $840 for five-piece set, *from Art Reed/Sweetwater Glass, RD 1, Box 88, Delancey, NY 13752, 914-676-4622.*

PAGE 112
Figs on the branch (prices vary by length), *from Green Valley Growers, 10450 Cherry Ridge Road, Sebastopol, CA 95472, 707-823-5583.*

Four-inch-wide **ribbon,** $8 per yard, *at Bell'occhio, 8 Brady Street, San Francisco, CA 94103, 415-864-4048; or contact Midori Inc., 3827 Stone Way North, Seattle, WA 98103, 206-547-9553 for retail information.*

PAGE 113
Small oval **baker's molds** (for gingerbreads), $8 each; *from Williams-Sonoma, 800-541-2233.*

PAGE 114
Venetian **glasses,** $195 for set of six, *from Tail of the Yak, 2632 Ashby Avenue, Berkeley, CA 94705, 510-841-9891.*

PAGE 115
Antique blown-glass **candlesticks,** $1,950 for pair; small **cut-crystal candlesticks,** $885 for pair; small **tinted cut-crystal candlesticks,** $450 for pair; pressed-glass **swirl-pattern candlesticks,** $480 for pair, *all from Marvin Alexander Inc., 315 East 62nd Street, New York, NY 10021, 212-838-2320.* Glass **compote dish,** $130, *from Art Reed/Sweetwater Glass, RD 1, Box 88, Delancey, NY 13752, 914-676-4622.*

PAGE 117
Audubon **flatware** by Tiffany & Co., $15,000 for service for twelve, *from Argentum, 414 Jackson Street, #101, San Francisco, CA 94111, 415-296-7757.*

Art-deco **tablecloth and napkins,** *from Linda Cheverton Art & Antiques, Box 53, Colebrook, CT 06021,*

203-379-5345.

PAGE 118, 119, 120

Dried lemons and limes *from Freeze-Dried Botanicals, 206 Ross Road, Suite 105A, King of Prussia, PA 19406, 215-992-9832. Call or write for nearest retailer.* **Dried oranges,** $10.50 per dozen; **sycamore balls,** $7.50 per dozen; **dried pomegranates,** $21 per dozen; *all from the Galveston Wreath Company, 800-874-8597.*

Metallic **crinkle wire,** $3 for three meters, *from D. Blümchen & Co. Inc., Box 1210-M, Ridgewood, NJ 07451, 201-652-5595.*

Gold **braided cord** by Brimar Inc. *Call Ursel Thiergart, 708-272-9585, for more information.* Three-eighths-inch-wide double-faced **satin ribbon,** $1 per yard, minimum mail order $20, *from Hyman Hendler & Sons, 67 West 38th Street, New York, NY 10018, 212-840-8393.*

Luminescent **organdy ribbon,** $2-$3 per yard, *from Bell'occhio, 8 Brady Street, San Francisco, CA 94103, 415-864-4048; or contact Midori Inc., 3827 Stone Way North, Seattle, WA 98103, 206-547-9553 for retail information.*

Silver and gold **metal beads,** $2.49 for one hundred ($25 minimum), *from Shipwreck Beads, 5021 Mud Bay Road, Olympia, WA 98502, 206-866-4061.*

Daisy **upholstery tacks,** $5 for one hundred ($25 minimum charge), *from BZI Distributors Corp., 105 Eldridge Street, New York, NY 10002, 212-966-6690.* **Hot-glue gun,** $10; **cup hooks,** $1 for package of six, *both from Kmart. Call 800-635-6278 for information.*

PAGE 121

Brass-mesh leaves, *special order from Dulken & Derrick Inc., 12 West 21st Street, New York, NY 10010, 212-929-3614.*

NEW YEAR'S EVE

PAGE 123

Decoration, clothing appliqué, and tablecloth stenciling *by Marla Weinhoff Studio, 95 Horatio Street #319, New York, NY 10014.*

PAGE 125

DEKA permanent fabric paint, $2.25 for one ounce, *from Decart Inc., 802-888-4217.*

The Index

RECIPES INDEXED BY CATEGORY

If you have enjoyed reading and using
THE BEST OF MARTHA STEWART LIVING:
HOLIDAYS
please join us as a subscriber to
MARTHA STEWART LIVING,
the magazine.
Simply call toll-free 1-800-999-6518.
The annual subscription rate is
$24 for 10 issues.